Woo[illegible] Toys: Projects and Plans

Home Craftsman Series

Heinz Graesch

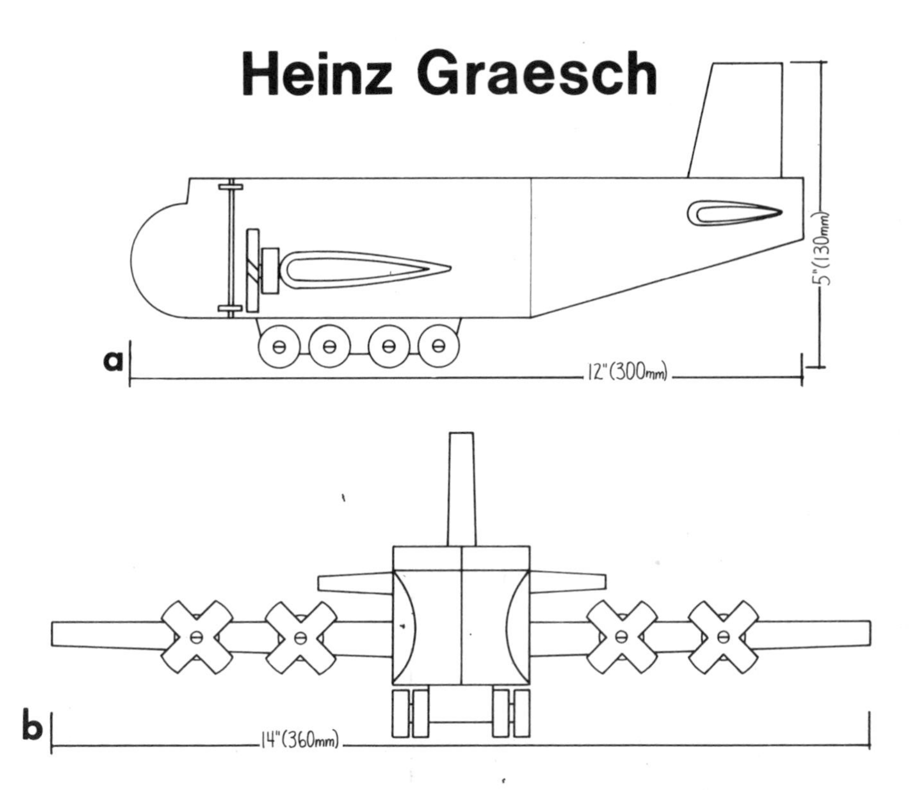

Sterling Publishing Co., Inc. New York

Distributed in the U.K. by Blandford Press

Translated by Michael Simon

Library of Congress Cataloging in Publication Data
Graesch, Heinz.
Wooden toys.
(Home craftsman series)
Translation of: Spielzeug aus Holz leicht gebaut, and selections from Holzarbeiten dekorativ und nützlich.
Includes index.
1. Wooden toy making. I. Graesch, Heinz. Holzarbeiten dekorativ und nützlich. English. Selections. 1983.
II. Title. III. Series.
TT174.5.W6G713 1983 745.592 83-4747
ISBN 0-8069-7606-3 (pbk.)

5 7 9 11 13 15 14 12 10 8 6 4

Two Park Avenue, New York. N.Y. 10016
The material in this book was originally published in Germany under the titles, "Spielzeug aus Holz leicht gebaut," and "Holzarbeiten dekorativ und nützlich," © 1974 and 1980, respectively, by Verlagsgesellschaft Rudolf Müller, Köln-Braunsfeld.
Distributed in Australia by Oak Tree Press Co., Ltd.
P.O. Box K514, Haymarket, Sydney 2000. N.S.W.
Distributed in the United Kingdom by Blandford Press
Link House, West Street, Poole, Dorset BH15 ILL, England
Distributed in Canada by Oak Tree Press Ltd.
% Canadian Manda Group, P.O. Box 920, Station U
Toronto, Ontario, Canada M8Z 5P9
Manufactured in the United States of America

Contents

Tools and Techniques

Following are descriptions of woodworking tools and techniques along with symbols for each. At the beginning of each project you will find the symbols for the tools and techniques you will need to complete construction.

Sawing with Handsaws

There are two basic kinds of handsaws: cross-cut saws for cutting across the grain and rip saws for cutting with (along) the grain. Saw teeth can be coarse or fine. A fine-tooth blade with 7 to 12 teeth to the inch (25 mm) is best for cross cuts. For most work, a blade with 7 or 8 teeth ("points") is best. Coarse blades intended for long cuts have $5\frac{1}{2}$ or $6\frac{1}{2}$ teeth per inch (25 mm). Saw teeth are usually arranged to point alternately outwards to opposite sides of the blade. This produces a cut slightly wider than the body of the blade, allowing it to pass freely through the wood.

There are also compass saws and keyhole saws with narrow, tapered blades for sawing curves and circles. You can cut areas out of the middle of a board by first making a drill hole in the material to be removed. The smaller the blade, the greater the maneuverability. The saws intended for longer cuts have thicker blades which hold the direction better.

As with all tools, a little maintenance goes a long way. Saws must be sharp. The teeth on a dull blade appear rounded and shiny. A little oil wiped on the blade before storage will protect it from rust and help it pass more freely through the wood. If the blade does become rusty, you can clean it off with steel wool.

Sawing with the Coping Saw

This saw is used to make curved cuts in wood that is not too thick. The adjustable blade allows you to saw curves of very small diameter. You can use a coping saw to cut sections out of the middle of a board.

Coping-saw blades are fragile and break easily. Be sure to have spares on hand to avoid having to stop work for want of a blade.

Sawing with a Circular Saw

The circular saw is one of the most helpful tools for the woodworking home craftsman. Besides the inexpensive portable saws, heavy-duty table or bench saws with built-in motors are also available. These bench saws have either adjustable tables or blades which allow you to cut grooves of varying depths.

Blades for circular saws are made with various configurations of teeth for a variety of cutting jobs. Cutting plywood, hardboard, or across the grain of ordinary lumber calls for a blade with fine teeth. Hollow-ground blades make the smoothest cuts in both thick and thin materials.

When a circular saw blade needs sharpening, it is best to send it to a professional sharpener. If you try to do it yourself and leave some of the teeth longer than others, or don't get the alternating set just right, you may destroy the whole work.

Most circular saws have an adjustable base plate to allow for angle cuts and a rip fence for maintaining a straight cut down the length of the board. Each portable saw has a retractable blade guard that is absolutely necessary for safety reasons.

You must always be very careful when using a

circular saw. *Never use your fingers to guide small pieces of wood into a bench saw.* Please, always use another piece of wood (a "push stick") for this task.

Using the Electric Drill in Wood

For the home craftsman, the portable electric drill is one of the most versatile tools, with accessories available for sanding, sawing, polishing, screwdriving, and many other tasks.

Drill bits are available in a wide range of sizes. Use spiral-twist bits for small-diameter holes, spade bits for larger ones. Spade bits often have two small points at the edge that serve as precutters to avoid tearing the grain of the wood. Using a spade bit makes it possible to drill perfectly straight round holes with very little difficulty.

If your work must be smooth on both sides, run the bit in only until the very point of it comes through the bottom. Turn the piece over and, using the small hole as a guide, complete drilling from this opposite direction.

Optional stands are available for most electric drills enabling you to convert them into a type of drill press. These really ensure that holes are drilled straight and also allow you to overlap holes if necessary.

Sawing Holes with a Hole Saw

The hole saw is a special bit for use with your drill. It makes perfectly circular holes in wood.

Below the saw teeth is a regular spiral drill which serves as a center guide. The cut-out pieces therefore have a hole in the middle. Some hole-saw bits are available without the center guide, useful for those occasions when the cut-out pieces are more important than the hole, such as when you are making wheels for children's toys.

This kind of cutting is much easier with the optional drill stand described above. Use a piece of scrap wood beneath the piece you are drilling to prevent splintering at the bottom of the cut. Clamp both boards securely to the base of the drill stand.

Routing

The router is an effective tool for rounding, bevelling, or cutting profiles of various shapes along the edges of boards. Router motors run at a high rate of revolution, so it is very important to follow the manufacturer's safety directions. Most machines have transparent shields that contain the dust, but wearing safety goggles is a further protection.

Planing

At least two planes are necessary for woodworking—a block plane and a jack plane. You can do most smoothing and straightening with these two tools. The smaller block plane can be used for planing across the grain at the end of a board. The adjustable blade can be set for very fine shaving, which is useful in trimming wood to size. The longer jack plane is best for straightening or trimming the edges of boards. Planing with this tool should always be done with (along) the grain of the wood.

A sharp edge is essential for clean planing. Previously, blade sharpening was done on a wet grindstone. Today, motor-powered grinding wheels are used. When using a grinder, do not press the blade too hard against the revolving wheel or the metal may become so hot that it anneals and loses its hardness. To avoid this, cool the blade down occasionally during dry sharpening.

The grindstone leaves a burr on the edge of the blade that has to be removed. Pour a few drops of oil onto an oilstone for the final smoothing.

Turning

The essential woodturning tool is the lathe. For the home craftsman with limited space, multi-purpose power tools that include a woodturning attachment are available. Three basic kinds of chisels are needed for woodturning: the gouge for rough turning, the square chisel for smoothing the surface, and the skew chisel for parting.

Sandpaper can be used to finish the turning piece, but only after the chisel work is completed. During sanding, small sand particles get stuck in the wood surface. These particles will blunt the tools very quickly.

Safety is of paramount importance with the lathe. Protection for the eyes and hands is a must.

Dowelling

Dowels serve both to align a connection between two pieces of wood and to make that connection stronger. The dowel should be just a little shorter than the combined depth of the two dowel holes. A lengthwise groove down the edge of the dowel will permit more glue to remain in the connection and will also allow the surplus glue to escape when the dowel is knocked in. Apply glue just before inserting the dowels, then clamp the pieces together until the glue dries.

You can use the following method for aligning the dowel holes. Mark the drill holes on one board and knock in nails. Snip off the heads of the nails and put both work pieces together. The nails will mark the drill holes for the second piece. Remove the nails before drilling the holes.

Using Wood Screws

Screws have several advantages over nails. They may be easily withdrawn at any time without injury to the material. They also hold the wood more securely, can be easily tightened, and are generally neater in appearance.

Wood screws are available in a variety of materials, types of heads, and sizes. Always use a screwdriver that is the appropriate type and size for the screw head. An ill-fitting screwdriver may damage the slot and render the screw useless. At best, the wrong size screwdriver will make the job more difficult. At worst, it can slip and cause serious injury.

Nailing

A quick joining of two wood pieces may be made with nails, especially where the advantages of wood screws (see above) are unnecessary. Small-headed nails (brads) can be countersunk easily with a nail set. When filled with wood filler and sanded, the nail holes will be barely noticeable after finishing.

Glueing with PVA

PVA (polyvinyl acetate) is ready for use as is. A white liquid, it comes in cans, tubes, or flexible containers and doesn't have to be mixed. The glue is spread generously on one of the joining surfaces, and then the wood pieces are lightly clamped together in position. Setting times vary for the different brands, but twenty-four hours is usually best for maximum strength.

Surplus glue should be removed with a damp cloth before the glue sets, especially if the wood is going to be stained afterwards. Wood can only be stained if the pores are open. Glue clogs the pores.

Sanding

Sandpaper (glasspaper) comes in a variety of grits, from very fine to very coarse. The higher the number, the coarser the grit. For ease in handling, a block can be used to wrap the sandpaper around. Rounding the top edges of the block will provide a better grip.

If there is a lot of material to be worked, start with a coarse-grit sandpaper. As the process progresses, switch to finer grits. During the final stages, sand only in the direction of the grain to avoid leaving any sanding traces on the ends. The surface can be rinsed with water (which causes tiny wood grains on the surface to swell), dried, and fine-sanded as a final touch. It is necessary to dust off or vacuum the sanded surfaces as most finishing requires dust-free conditions.

Power Sanding

The often tedious chore of sanding has been made much easier by the advent of power tools. The two basic types of power sanders useful for the home craftsman are belt sanders, for heavy-duty sanding of large surfaces, and orbital sanders, for the final smoothing before finishing.

To avoid scratching or burning the wood surface, start the belt sander before applying it to the work. Likewise, lift the sander from the wood before turning it off. Similarly, don't tilt the sander, don't let it remain stationary, and don't exert undue pressure.

You can also buy a sanding plate for your electric drill or bench saw. Using a sanding plate on a bench saw allows you to do very exact work. The work piece goes on the sanding table which holds it at a very precise angle to the rotating disc.

Finishing

Select from among the wide variety of finishes by matching the appropriate qualities of the finishing material with the construction and intended use of the project. Heavy outdoor use, for example, requires a weatherproof finish. An attractive, fancy-grade wood should take a clear finish, while an opaque finish might be appropriate for lower grades or plywood. Since everything finds its way into a young child's mouth, you should avoid any finishes that are toxic, such as lead-based paint.

You may wish to consult one of the many good reference books covering all aspects of wood finishing. Be sure to follow the manufacturer's directions, especially concerning safety, as many finishes are flammable and some produce noxious fumes.

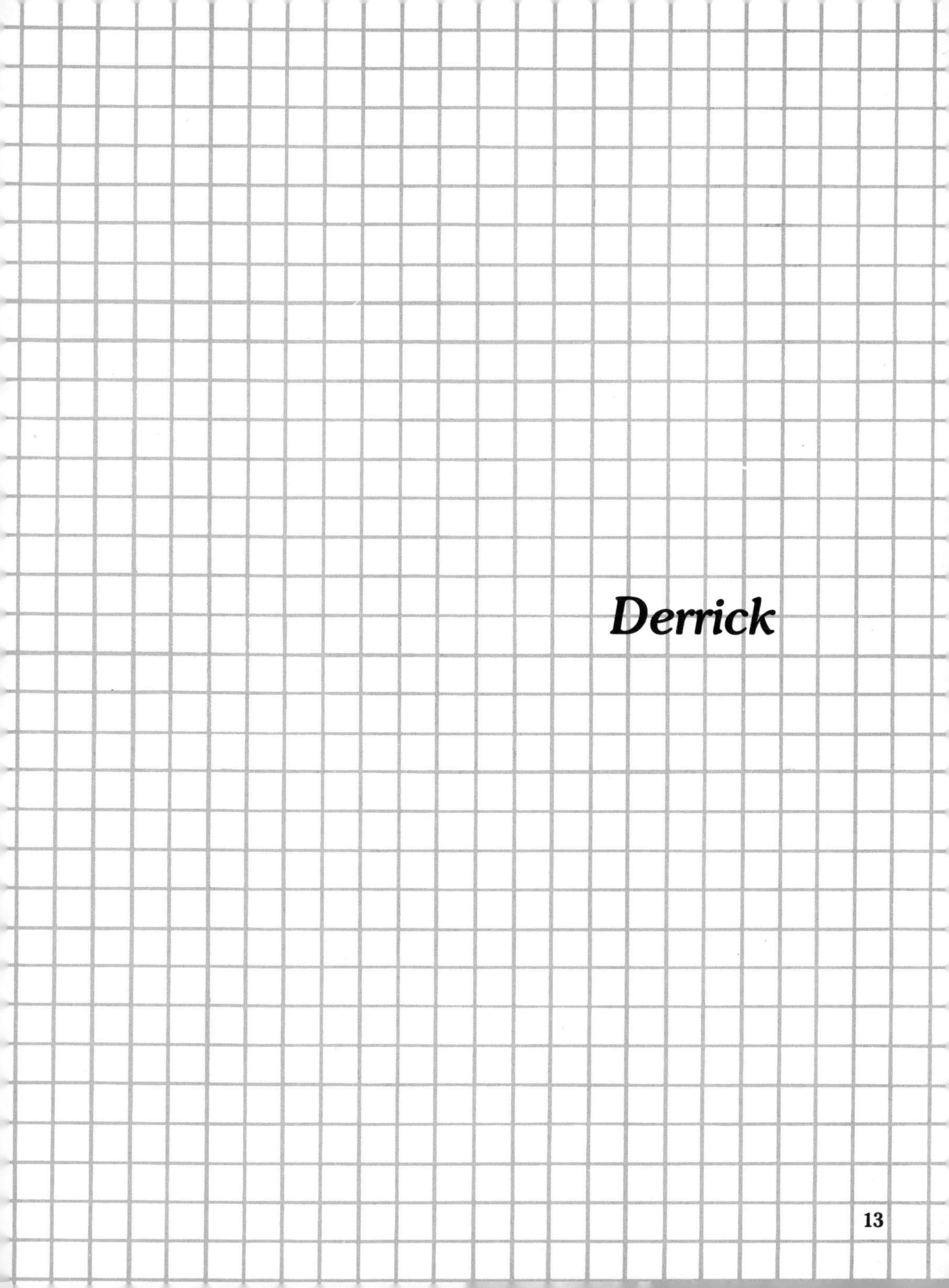

Derrick

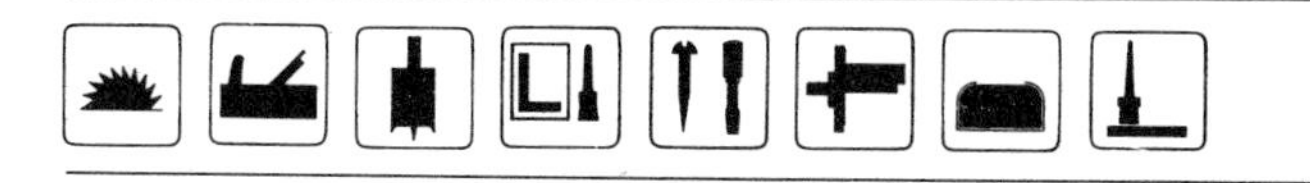

Derrick

The derrick consists of three major construction elements: the chassis; the mast with turntable; and the jib. Construct the components as follows.

Turn the wheels (**b**), which are attached directly to the chassis (**a**), from beechwood. The holes for the screws which hold the wheels to the chassis have to be slightly larger than the screws to allow the wheels to turn. Countersink the screw heads so that they are flush with the sides of the wheels by drilling a hole slightly wider than the screw head to the appropriate depth. Do the same for all other screw connections.

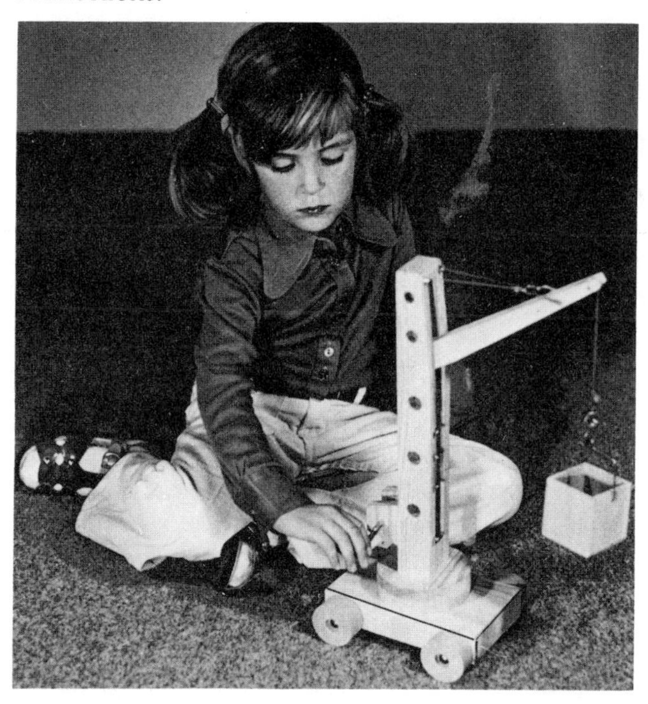

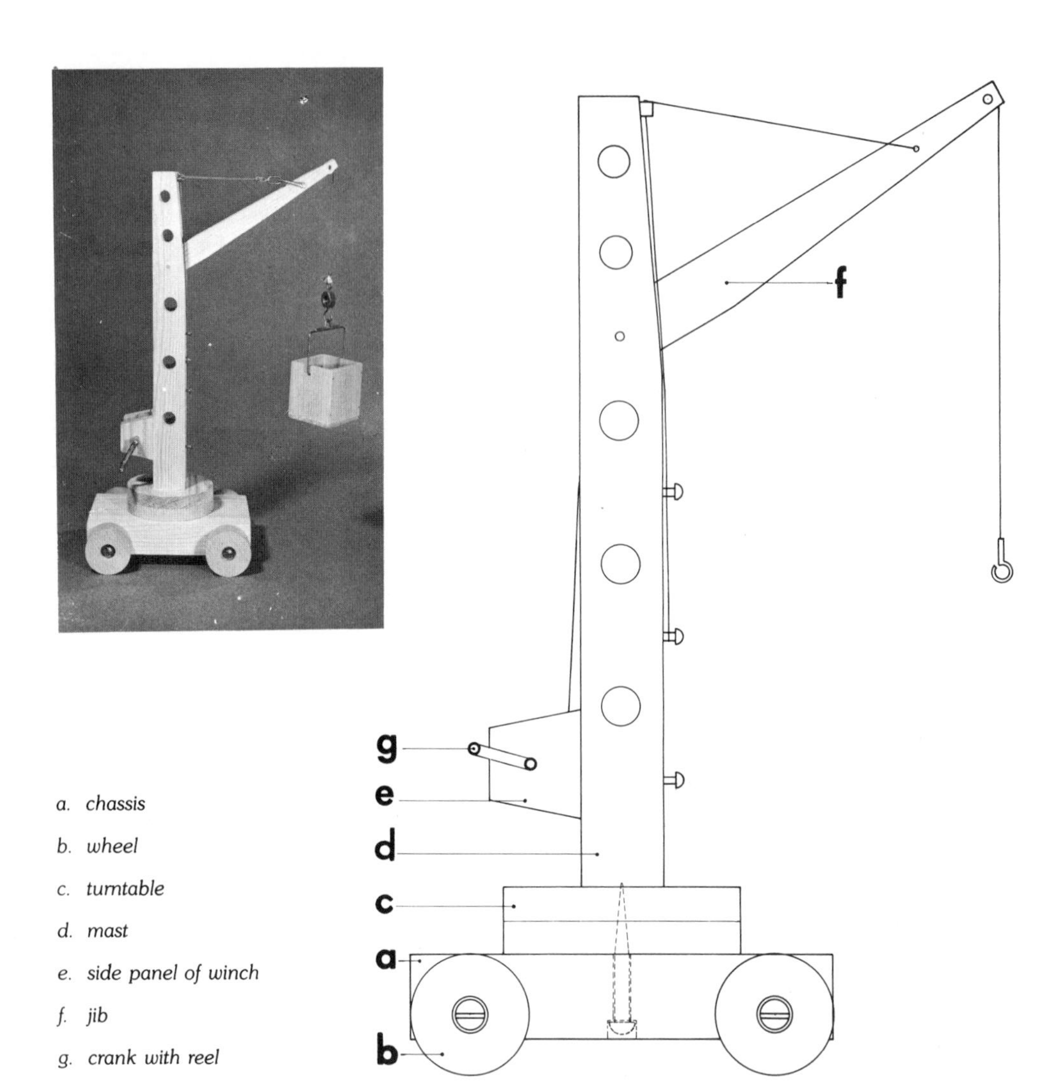

a. chassis

b. wheel

c. turntable

d. mast

e. side panel of winch

f. jib

g. crank with reel

Make the mast of two pieces joined together by two 1″ (24-mm) -thick pieces of wood glued between them at top and bottom as shown on the cross section **d**. The winch consists of two side panels (**e**) and the crank (**g**). Before fastening the side panels to the mast with screws as shown in **e**, you must first fit the reel and its axle into holes drilled in the side panels. The reel should fit tightly on the

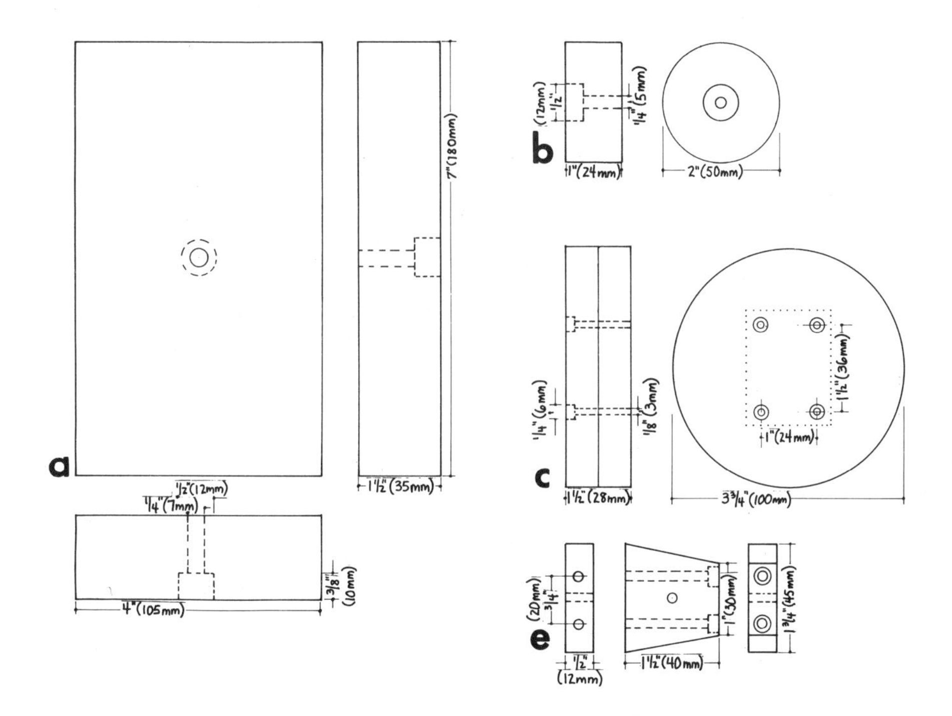

a. chassis

b. wheel

c. turntable

e. side panel of winch

axle. If you make the crank of wood, drill a small hole through the reel and axle and pass a split-pin through. Use the round end of the pin to hold the end of the cable.

Next, mount the bottom end of the mast on the turntable (**c**) which operates as a pivot by means of a large countersunk screw passing through from the chassis (**a**) into the mast.

Glue the two side pieces of the jib together with two $\frac{1}{4}$" (8 mm) -thick blocks of wood as shown in cross section **f**. Attach the jib to the mast with a piece of wooden dowel or metal rod. A small pulley goes on this axle, an even smaller one at the tip of the jib. You can make the pulleys of wood or buy them ready-made. Radio supply shops are a possible source of supply as such pieces are used in some radios.

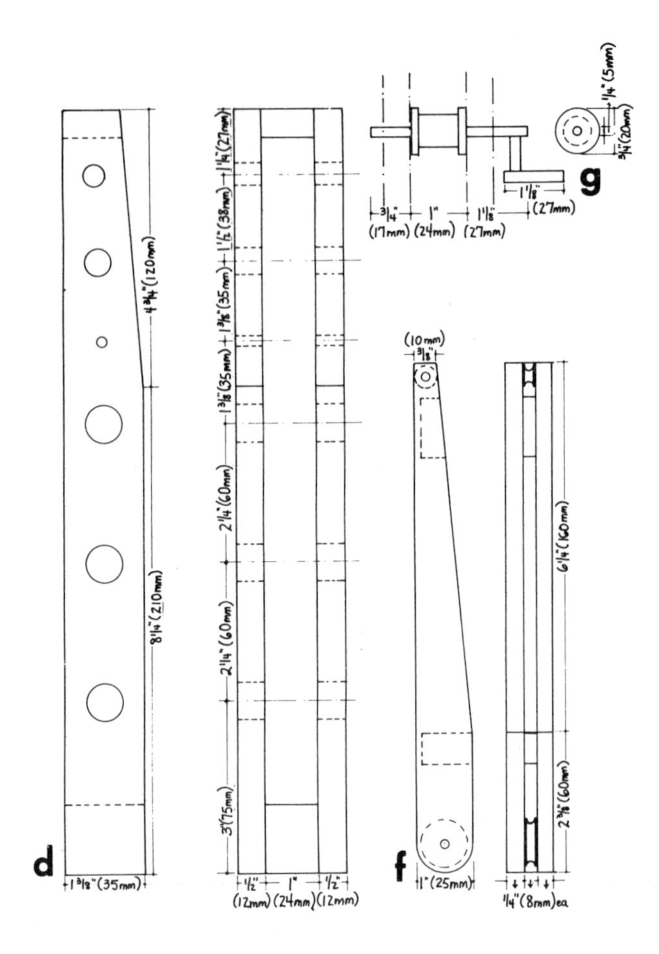

d. mast

f. jib

g. crank with reel

To provide a means of raising and lowering the jib, run a guy rope cord from a point near the end of it through a hole in the top block of the mast to be attached to nail heads at various heights on the mast as shown in the main side-view drawing. Finally, attach another cord to run from the reel over the two pulleys, ending with a heavy hook to hold the cable taut when not attached to a load.

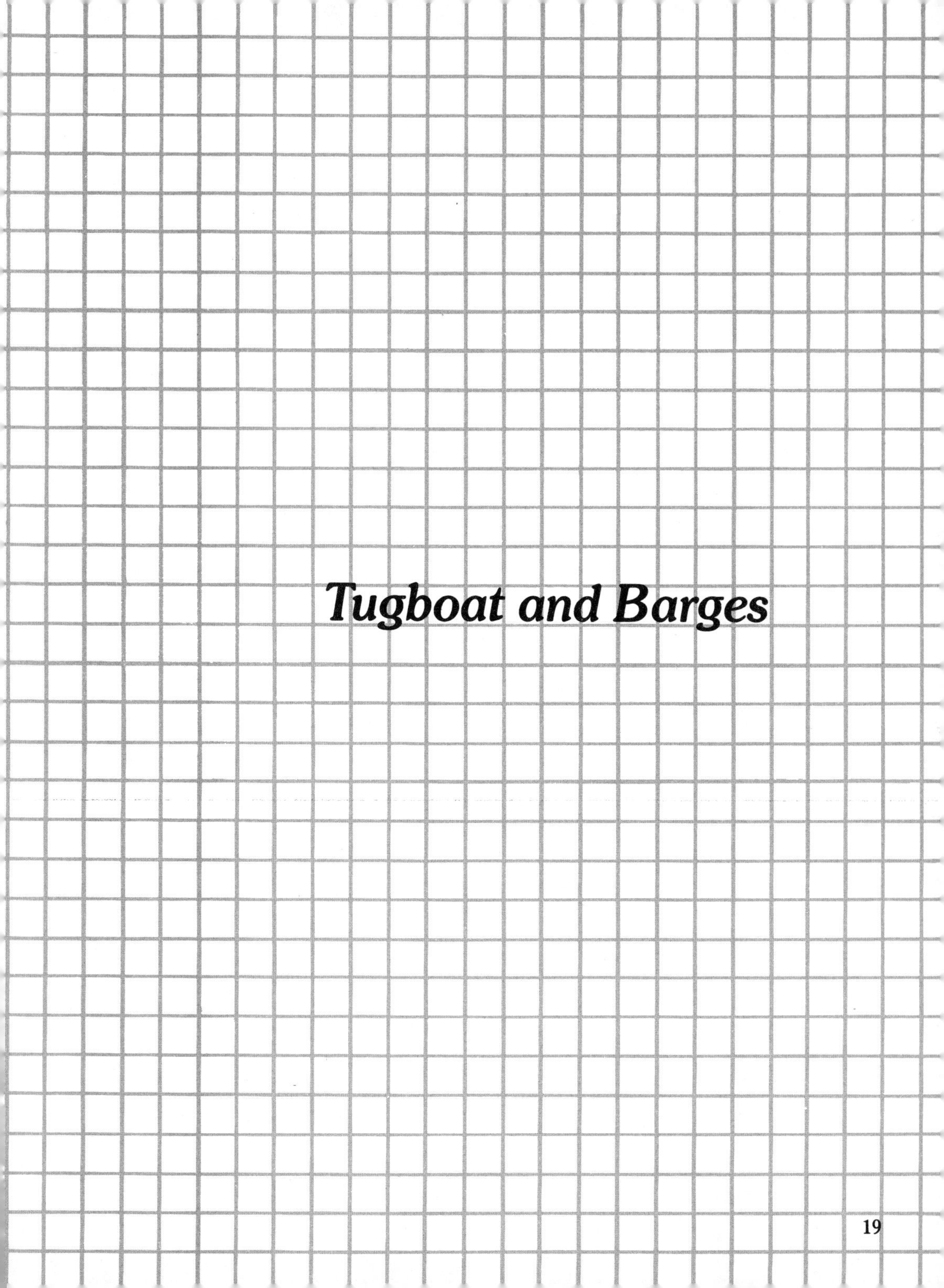

Tugboat and Barges

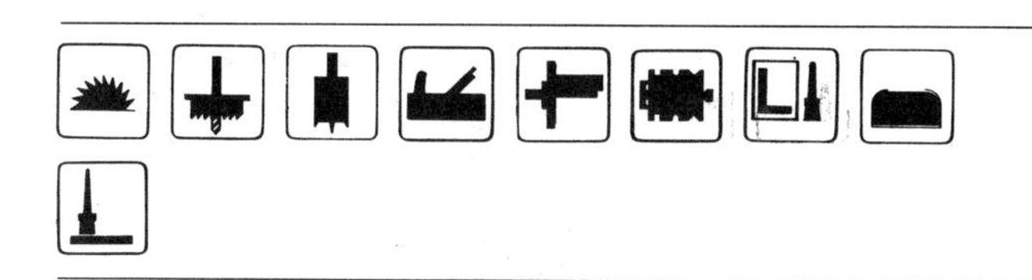

Tugboat and Barges

Make the hulls of the tugboat and barges from layers of $\frac{1}{2}''$ (13-mm) pine glued together. Each layer has the same outer dimensions (the tugboat, however, is shorter than the barge), so, instead of drawing the patterns over and over, make templates. Use a compass and ruler to draw the outer and inner (for the top layers) contours on cardboard. Use the templates to trace the outlines onto the wood.

For the tugboat you will need one **d** part and two **e** parts; for the barges, one **l** part and one **m** part. Glue the two **e** pieces together first and sand the inner edges before glueing them to the bottom piece (**d**). After the glue dries, sand the outer edge of the hull. Use the sander plate of your drill.

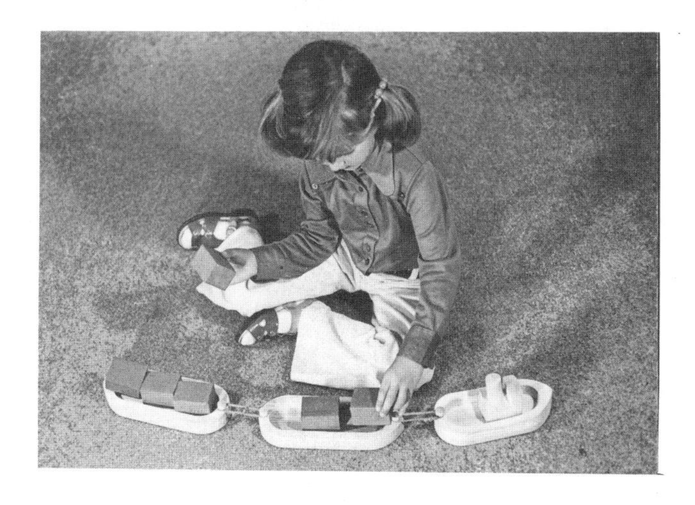

a. *side view tugboat*

b. *top view tugboat*

c. *front view tugboat*

h. *front view cabin*

i. *side view cabin*

j. *front view smokestack*

k. *side view smokestack*

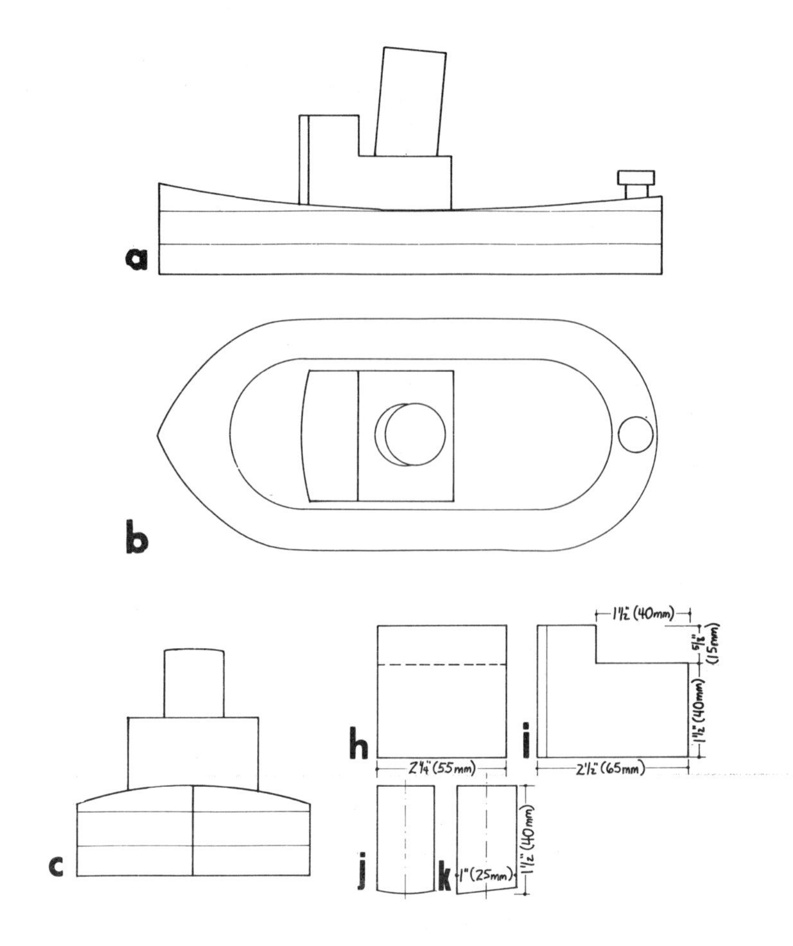

Cut away part of the top layer of the tugboat as shown in **a** and **g** so that the bow and stern are higher than the middle. Leave the barges flat.

The upper structure of the tugboat is made from pieces **h**-**i** and **j**-**k**, the cabin and stack. Shape the cabin from a pine block, the stack from a piece of dowel. The two are glued together first and then glued onto the base.

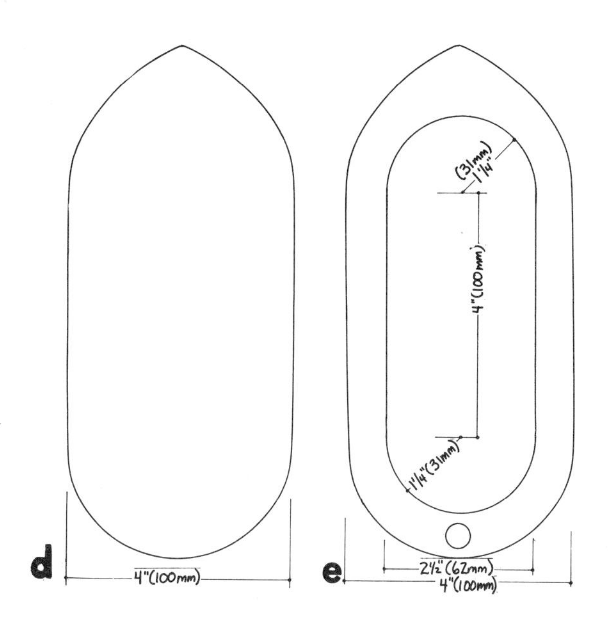

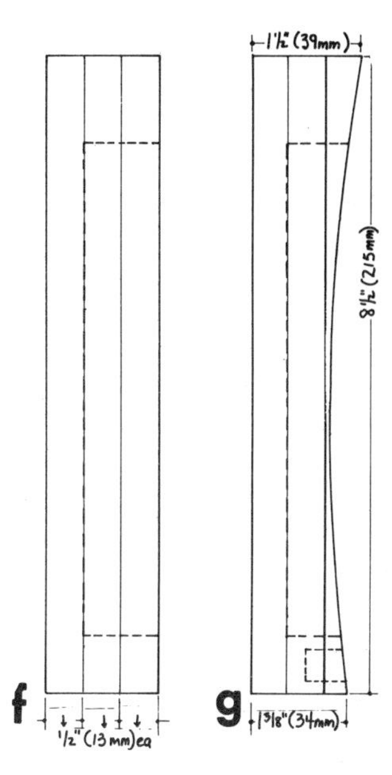

Fasten the tugboat and barges together by means of cords looped around posts. Turn the posts from beech and glue them into the holes where indicated on drawings **e** and **m**.

d. bottom layer tugboat

e. upper layer tugboat

f. side view joined layers

g. side view after shaping

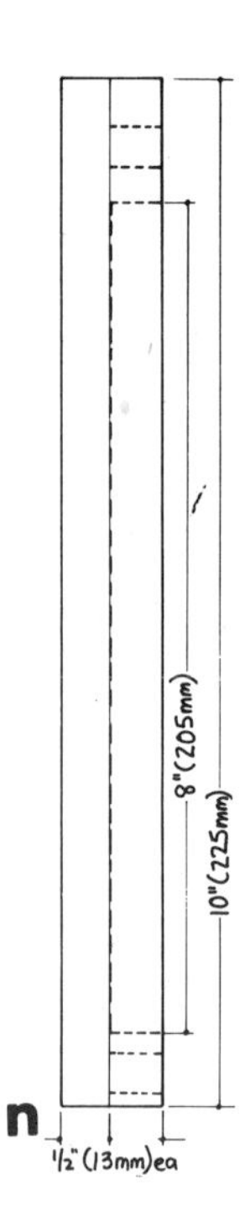

l. bottom pieces barge

m. top pieces barge

n. side view of joined pieces of barge

Because the boats may be used in water, you should finish the surface thoroughly. After priming, apply at least two coats of waterproof enamel (also called deck paint).

For security, you may want to use screws as well as glue to connect the layers of the hull.

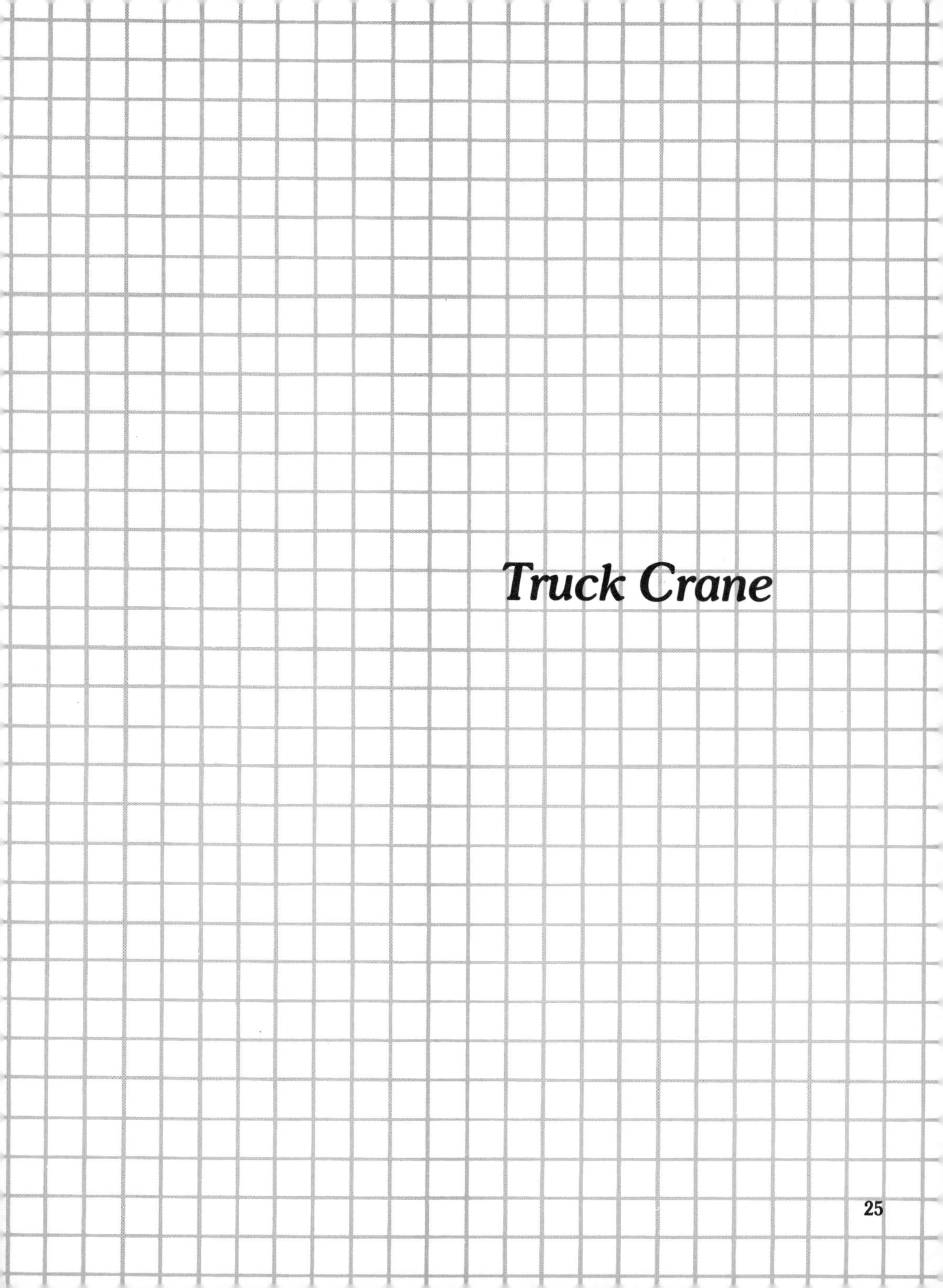

Truck Crane

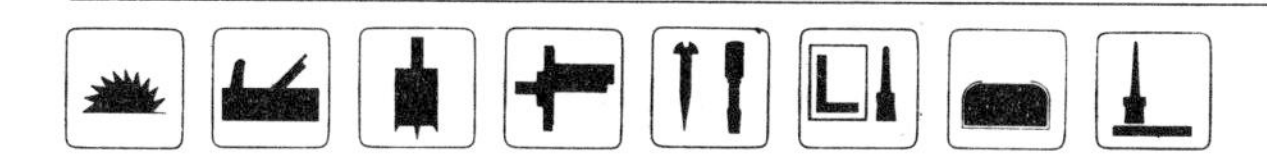

Truck Crane

Make the chassis **b** and the turntable **c** in the same way as those for the derrick on page 15.

The cab (**a**) is made from two thick pieces of wood with a thin piece between them, all glued together. (A block made in this way won't crack easily.) Bore a $1\frac{1}{8}''$ (30-mm) -wide hole through the cab (**a**) to accommodate the winch, which consists of the parts **i, k, j, l,** all made out of metal. The winch axle (**j**) turns in the holes in the side panels (**i**) which are attached on the outside. Solder a small loop on the axle to hold the hoisting rope (**m**). The set screw (**k**) on the crank (**l**) keeps the axle in place.

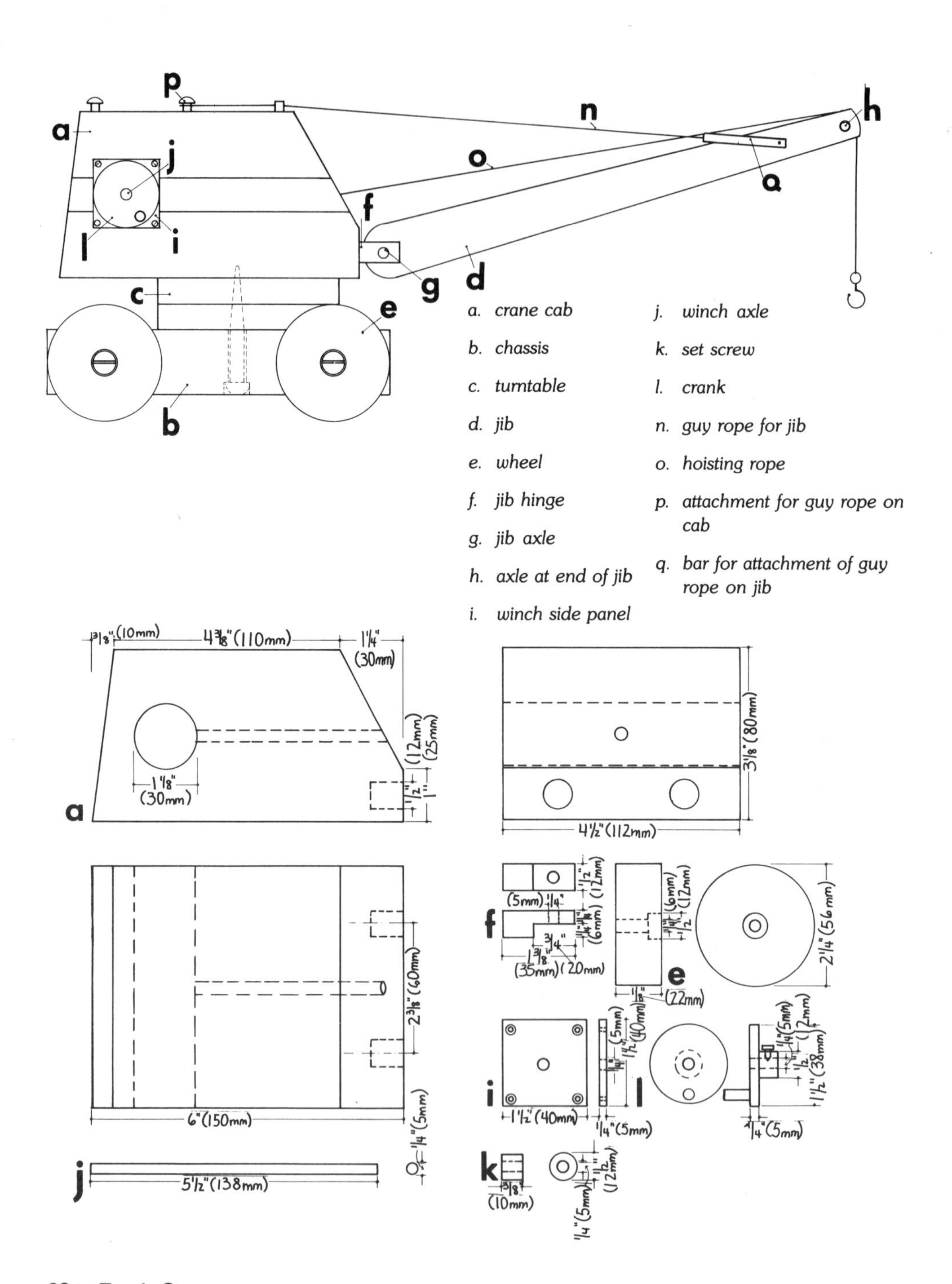
a. crane cab
b. chassis
c. turntable
d. jib
e. wheel
f. jib hinge
g. jib axle
h. axle at end of jib
i. winch side panel
j. winch axle
k. set screw
l. crank
n. guy rope for jib
o. hoisting rope
p. attachment for guy rope on cab
q. bar for attachment of guy rope on jib
3/8" (10mm)
4 3/8" (110mm)
1 1/4" (30mm)
(12mm)
(25mm)
1 1/8" (30mm)
1/2"
1"
3 1/8" (80mm)
4 1/2" (112mm)
2 3/8" (60mm)
6" (150mm)
1/4" (5mm)
5 1/2" (138mm)
(5mm) 1/4"
1/2" (12mm)
1/4" (6mm)
1 3/8" (35mm)
3/4" (20mm)
7/8" (22mm)
2 1/4" (56mm)
1 1/2" (40mm)
1/4" (5mm)
1 1/2" (38mm)
3/8" (10mm)
1/2" (12mm)

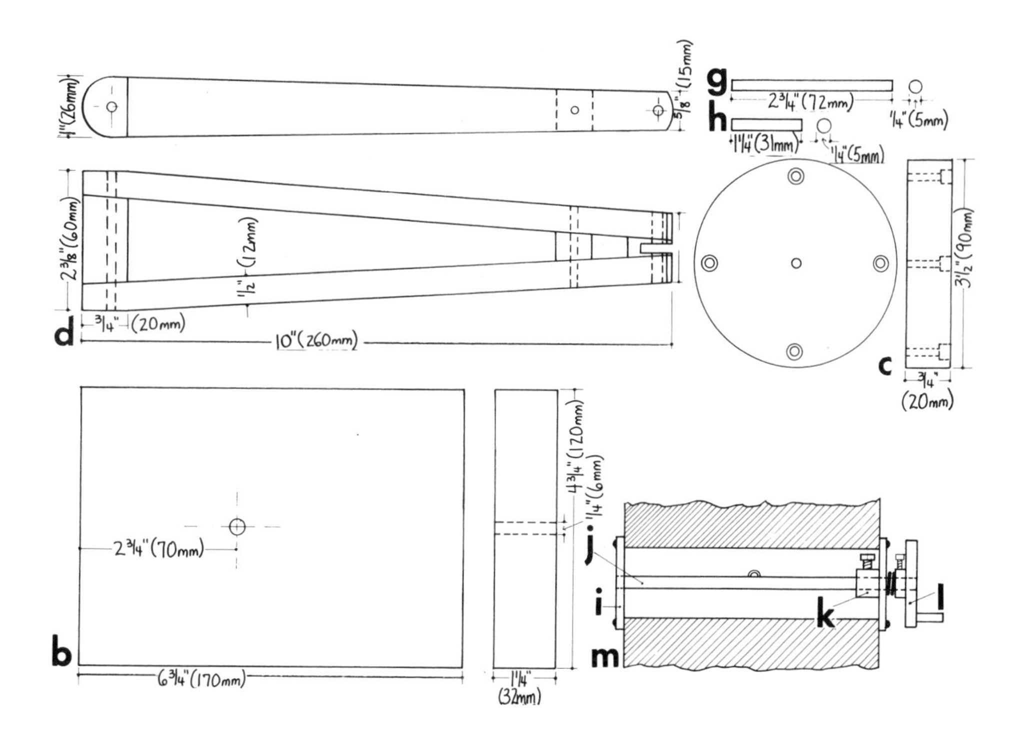

A small spring between the crank and the side panel ensures that the hoisting rope never unwinds by itself.

The hoisting rope (**o**) runs from the winch out of the cab through a $\frac{5}{16}$″ (8-mm) -wide hole drilled through the cab as shown in drawing **a**. The cord then passes over the reel at the end of the jib. The jib (**d**) is adjustable in height. A metal bar (**q**) on the end of the jib is the attachment for a guy rope running through a loop to screws (**p**) which are placed $1\frac{3}{4}$″ (45-mm) apart on the top of the cab.

Glue two pieces of beechwood, $\frac{1}{2}$″ (12 mm) thick, to the front of the cab to serve as hinges (**f**) for the jib. Shape the parts as shown in plan **f**. The axle of the jib is a $\frac{3}{16}$″ (5-mm) metal rod (**g**).

b. chassis

c. turntable

d. jib

g. jib axle

h. axle at end of jib

i. winch side panel

j. winch axle

k. set screw

l. crank

m. detail of winch

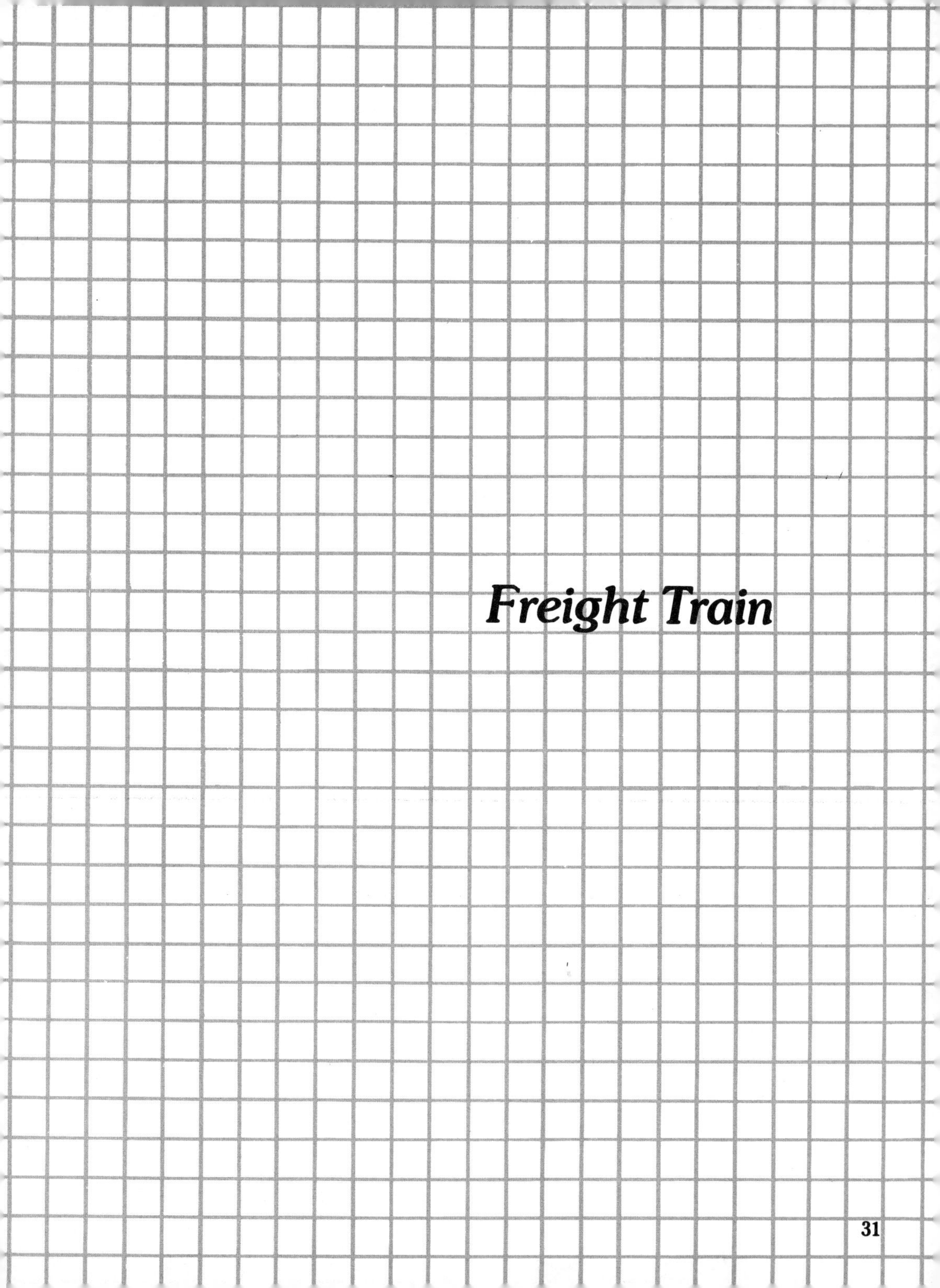

Freight Train

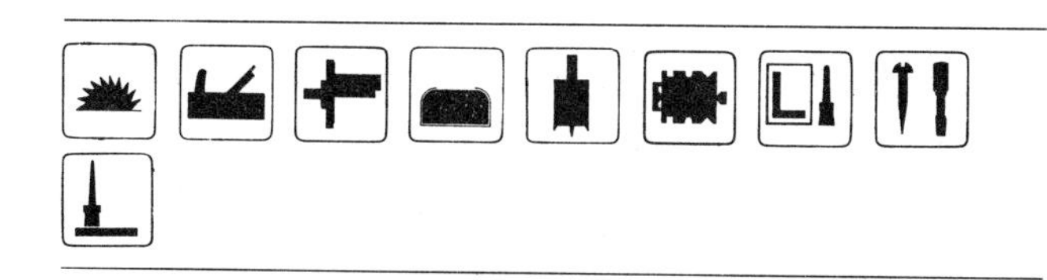

Freight Train

The steam locomotive and the freight cars have wheels (**d**) made of beech. You can turn the wheels on a lathe. If one is not available, saw out the wheels from a $\frac{1}{2}$" (12-mm) -thick beech board. Round them off completely on the sanding plate of your drill.

Fasten the wheels to the base of the locomotive as shown in drawing **e**.

The base or platform of the locomotive (**j**) is $3\frac{1}{2}$" × 6" × $\frac{1}{2}$" (90 × 150 × 14 mm). For the boiler (**k**) glue two thick boards together, then round

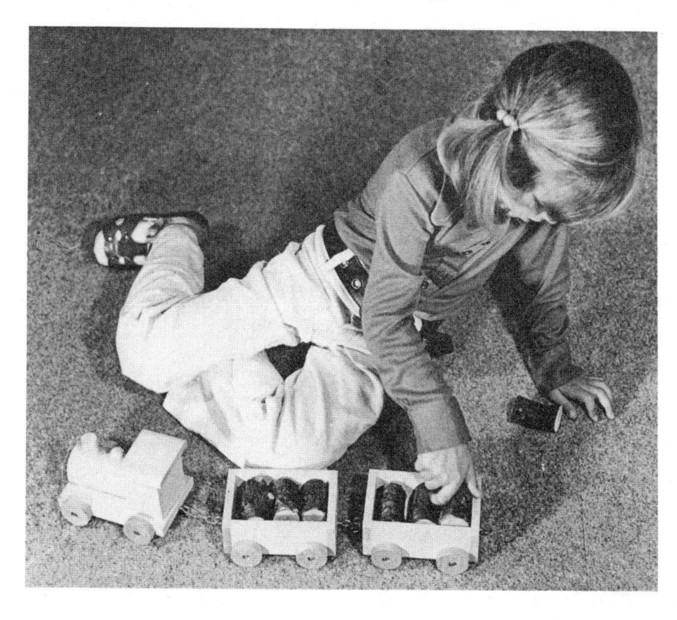

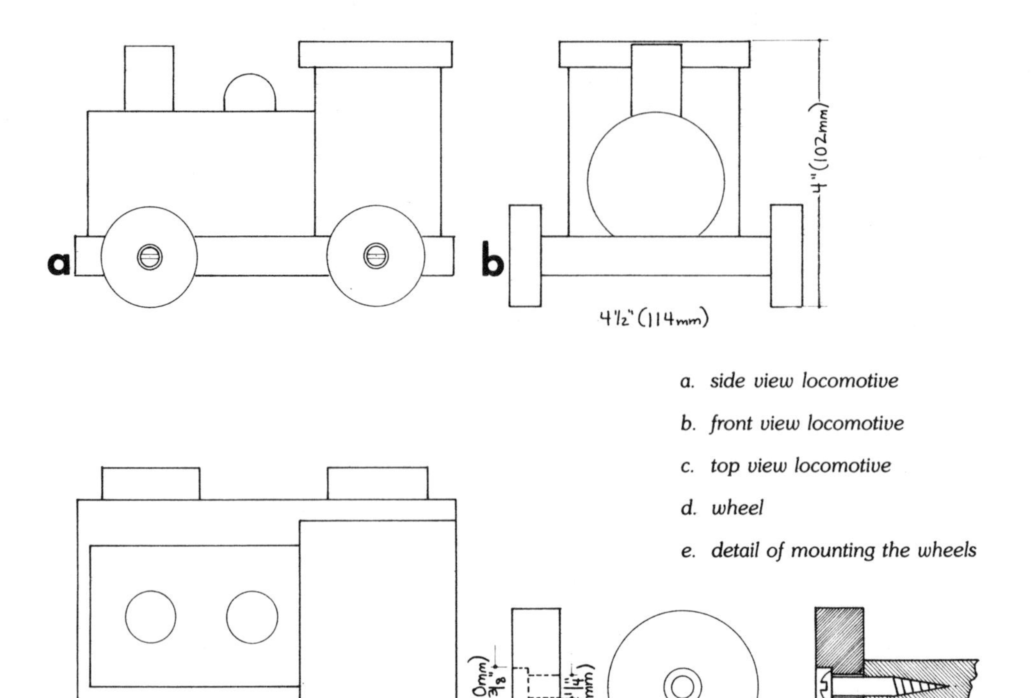

a. *side view locomotive*

b. *front view locomotive*

c. *top view locomotive*

d. *wheel*

e. *detail of mounting the wheels*

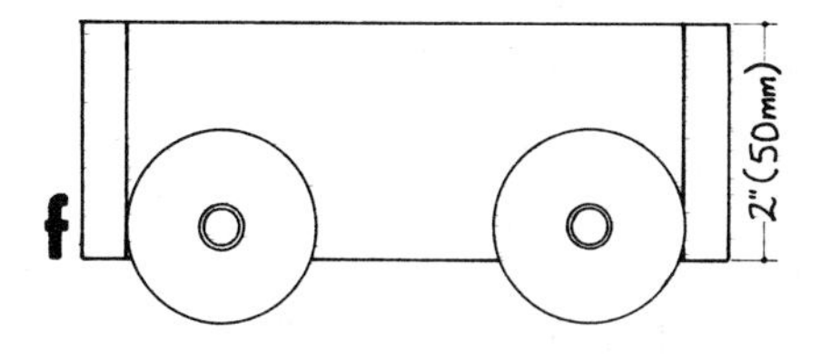

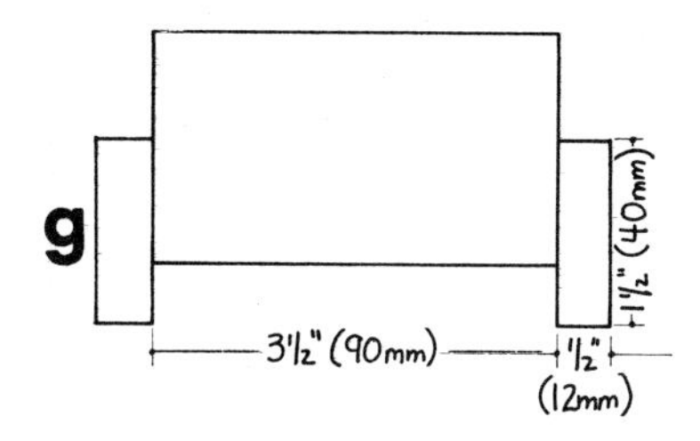

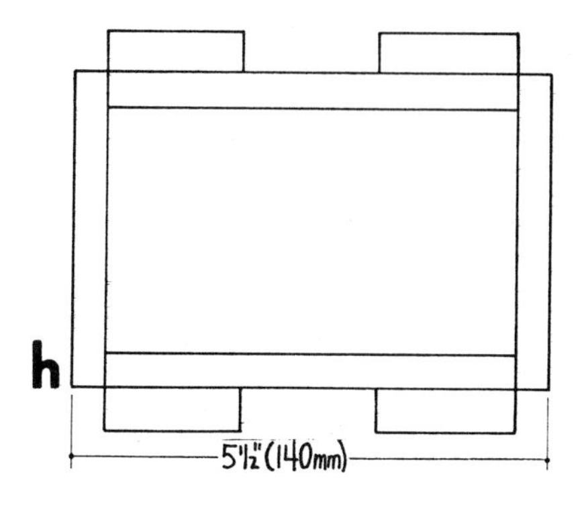

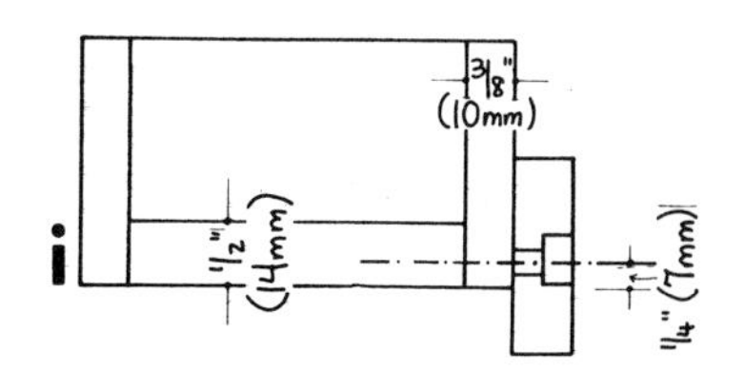

them. Flatten the bottom of the boiler as shown before screwing it to the platform.

Drill two holes in the boiler to hold the smoke-stack (**n**) and the steam dome (**o**), and glue the finished pieces into them.

Make the engineer's cab (**l**) out of one block of wood with a $\frac{3}{8}$″ (10-mm) -thick top (**m**) which is glued on.

The bottom pieces of the cars are $\frac{1}{2}$″ (14 mm) thick. The side panels are $\frac{3}{8}$″ (10 mm) thick. First, glue the bottom piece and the side panels together. After the glue is dry, sand the front edges smooth, then glue the front and back panels on. After that, when they are thoroughly dry, sand all edges and the bottom.

Screw the wheels (**d**) of the cars through the

f. side view freight car

g. front view freight car

h. top view freight car

i. detail of mounting the wheels on the car

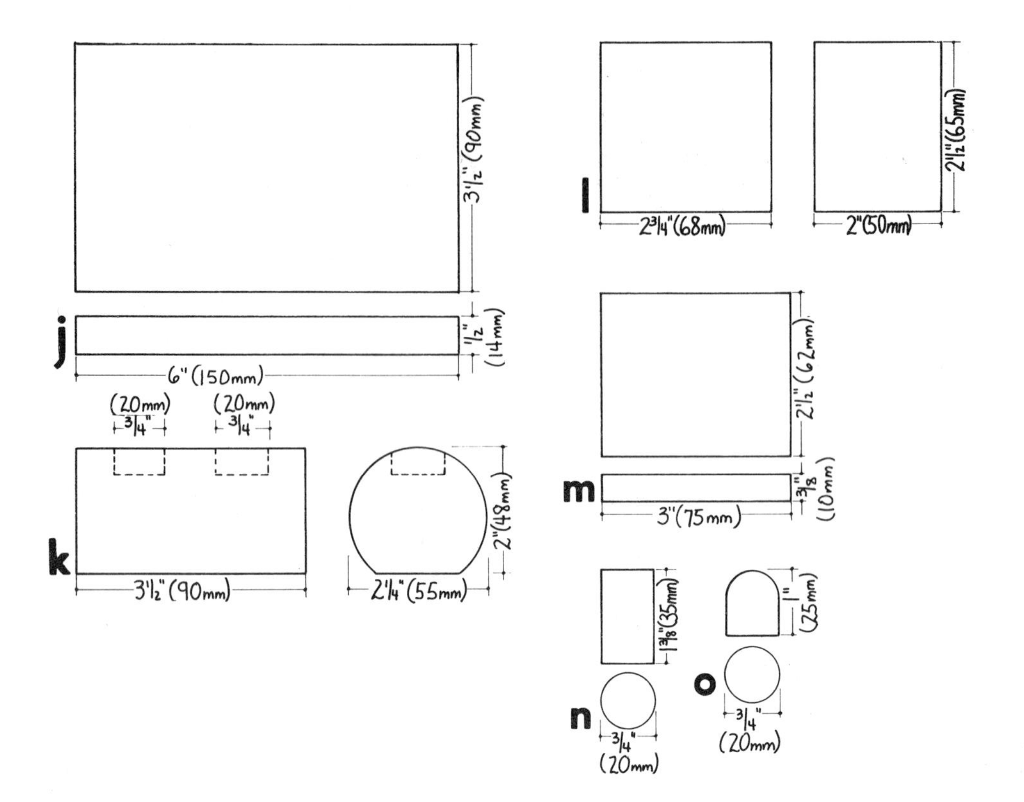

j. platform of locomotive

k. boiler

l. engineer's cab

m. top of cab

n. smokestack

o. steam dome

side panels into the bottom piece as indicated in drawing **i**.

To connect the locomotive and the cars, use screw hooks. The actual hook-up is made with three links of metal chain (see photo on page 34).

Steam Roller

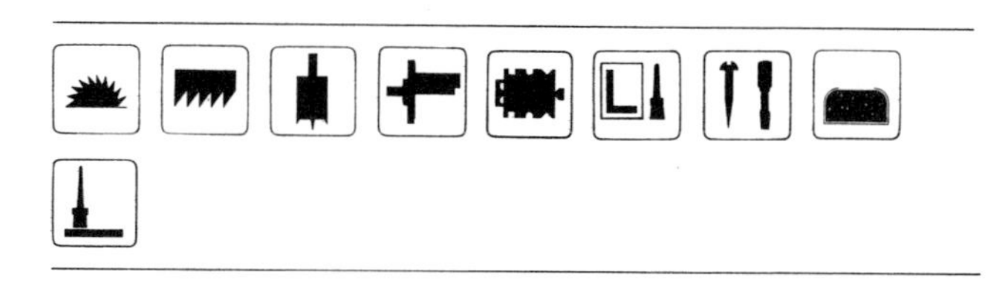

Steam Roller

The main body section (**d**) is 2″ (48 mm) thick. Saw it out of a single thick piece of wood if it is available. Otherwise, you can glue two pieces together.

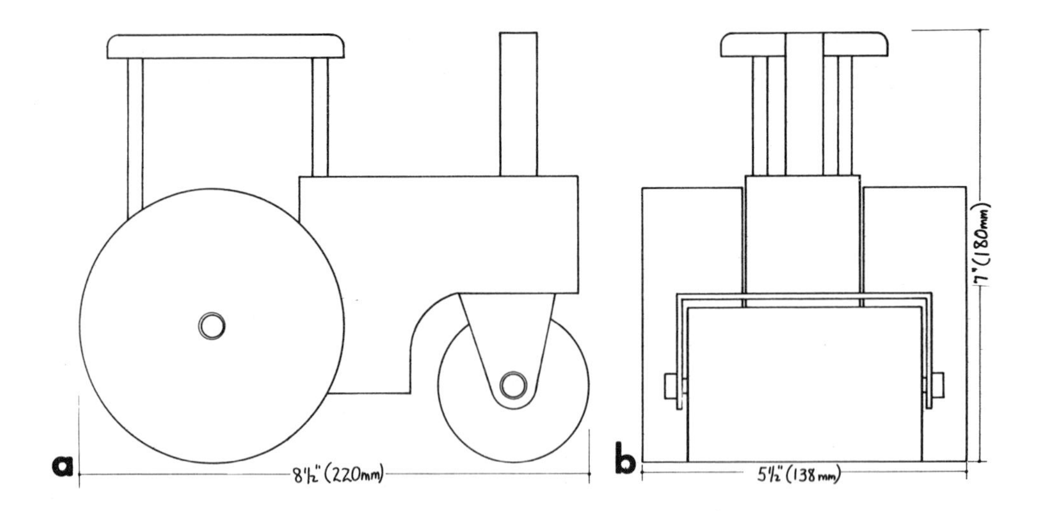

a. side view

b. front view

After cutting out the correct shape and sanding the edges, mark out and drill holes as follows. The hole for the rear axle is ¼" (6 mm) in diameter. Drill four ¼" (6-mm) holes for the dowels (**h**, **i**) supporting the top, and one additional hole, ¾" (20 mm) in diameter, for the smokestack (**j**).

Turn the roller (**e**) and the rear wheels (**f**) from beechwood on the lathe. Here again, if need be, you can use a few boards glued together to achieve the necessary thickness.

Use a ¼" (6-mm) metal rod for the axles for the roller and wheels. Use a metal cap on each end of the axle. The caps can be countersunk below the surface of the wheels. Be sure to allow enough space on the axle for the wheels and roller to turn freely.

The roller fits into a bracket (**k**) made of 1/16" (2-mm) -thick metal. After drilling the two ¼" (6-mm) holes for the axle, make four holes for attaching the roller support to the body as shown on drawing **k**. Paint the metal pieces and attach it to the body.

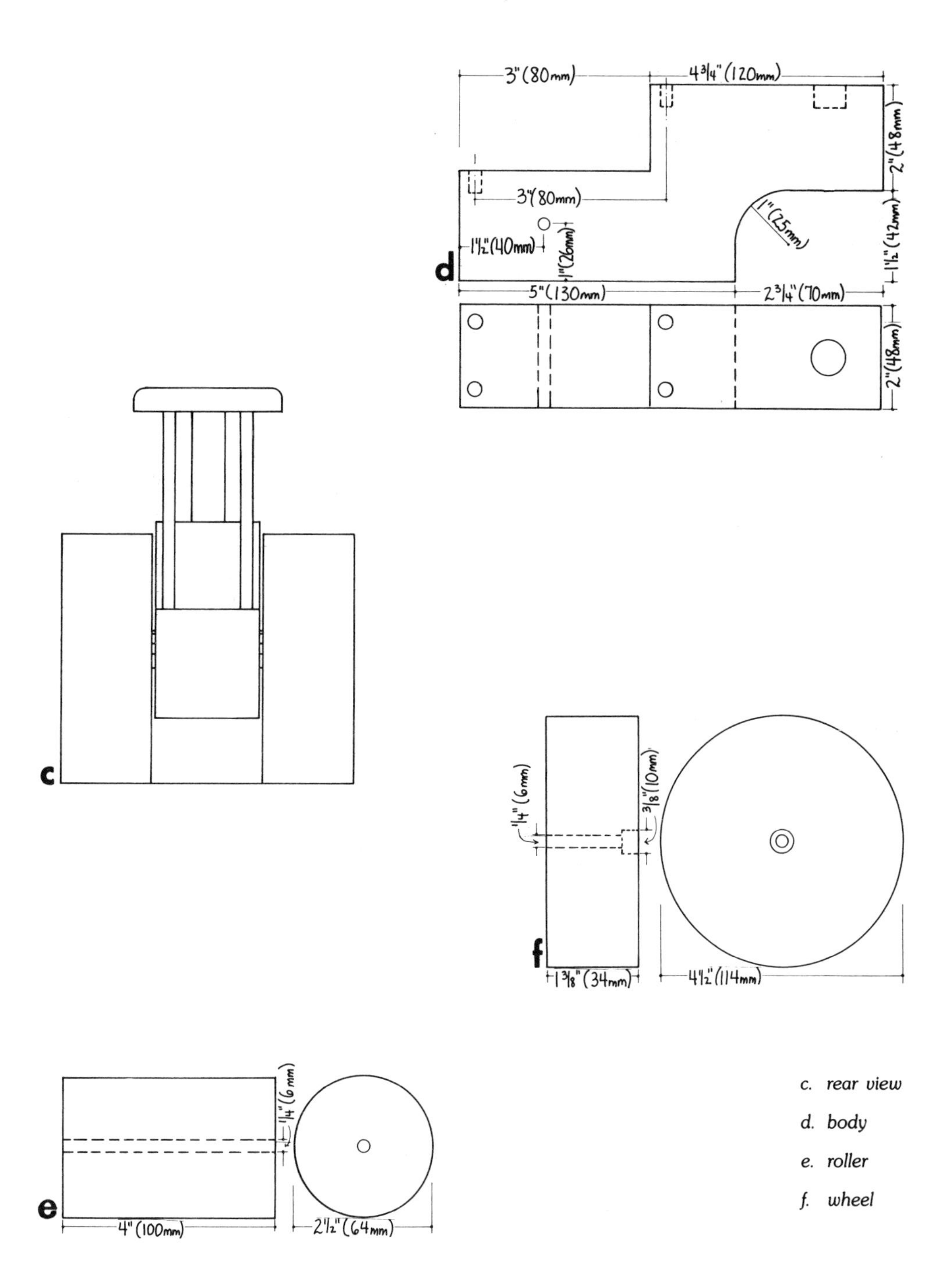

c. rear view

d. body

e. roller

f. wheel

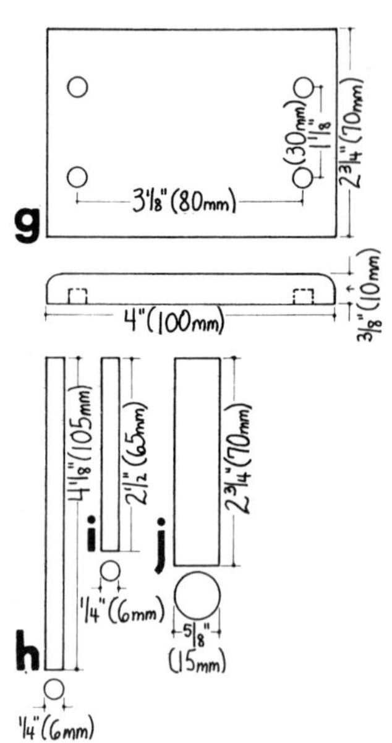

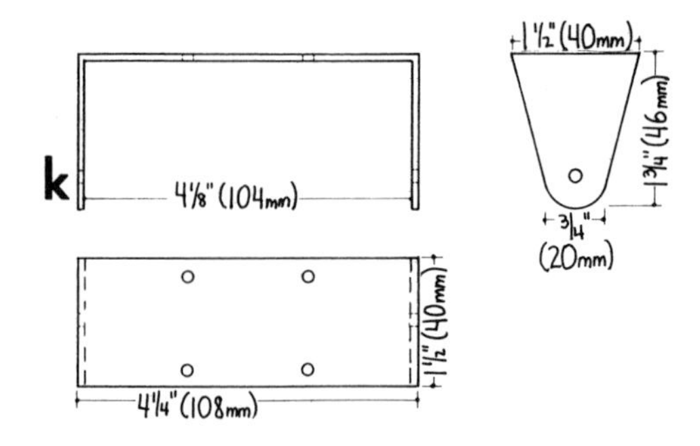

Glue the dowel supports for the roof (**h** and **i**) into the holes in the body (**d**) and then glue the roof on top.

Finally, glue the smokestack (**j**), made from ⅝" (15-mm) -thick dowel into the hole in the top of the body (**d**).

g. roof

h. rear roof supports

i. front roof supports

j. smokestack

k. metal bracket for roller

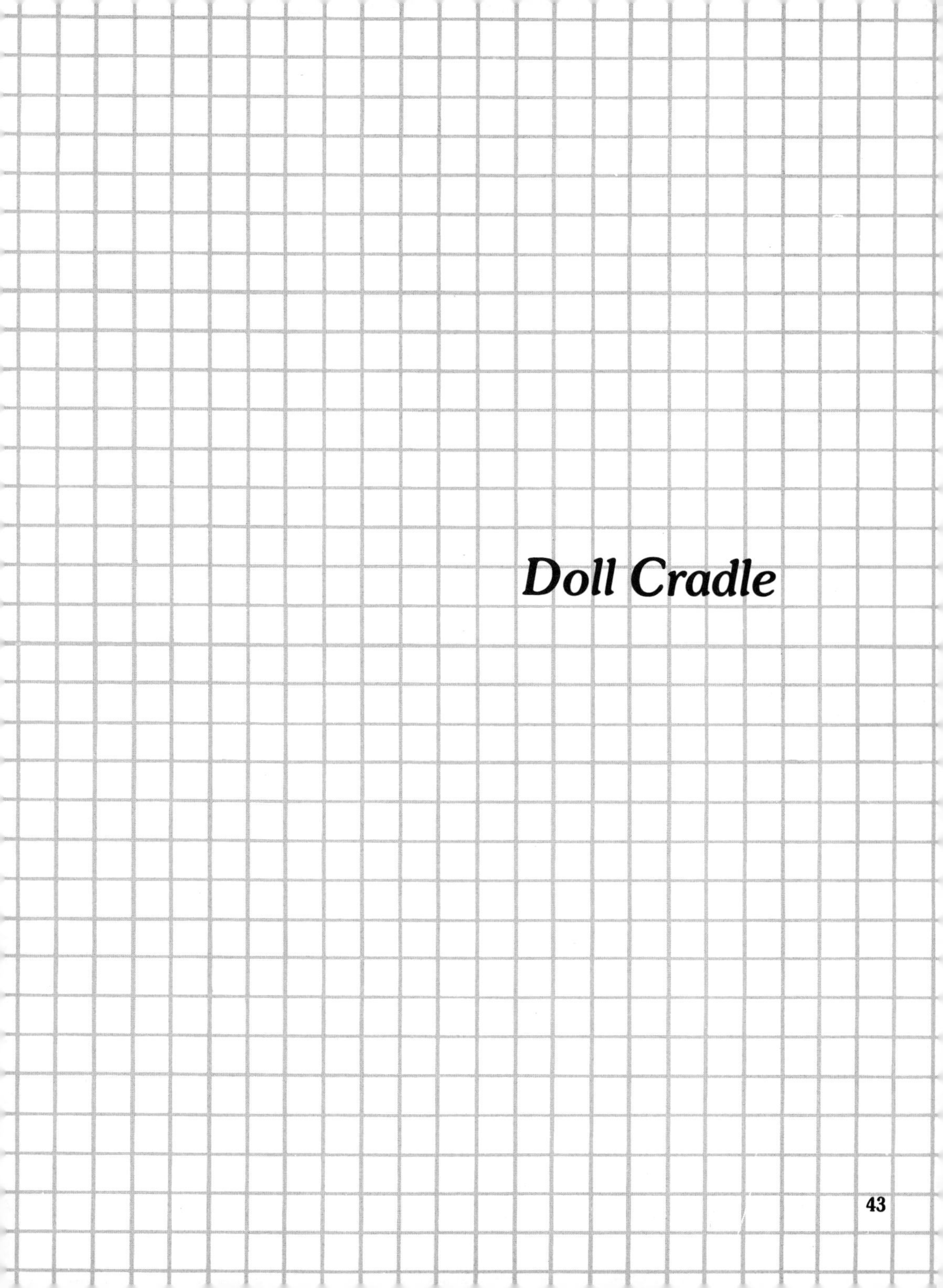

Doll Cradle

Doll Cradle

For the simple, peasant-style doll cradle shown in the photograph, you will need ¼″ (5-mm) -and ⅜″ (8-mm) -thick plywood.

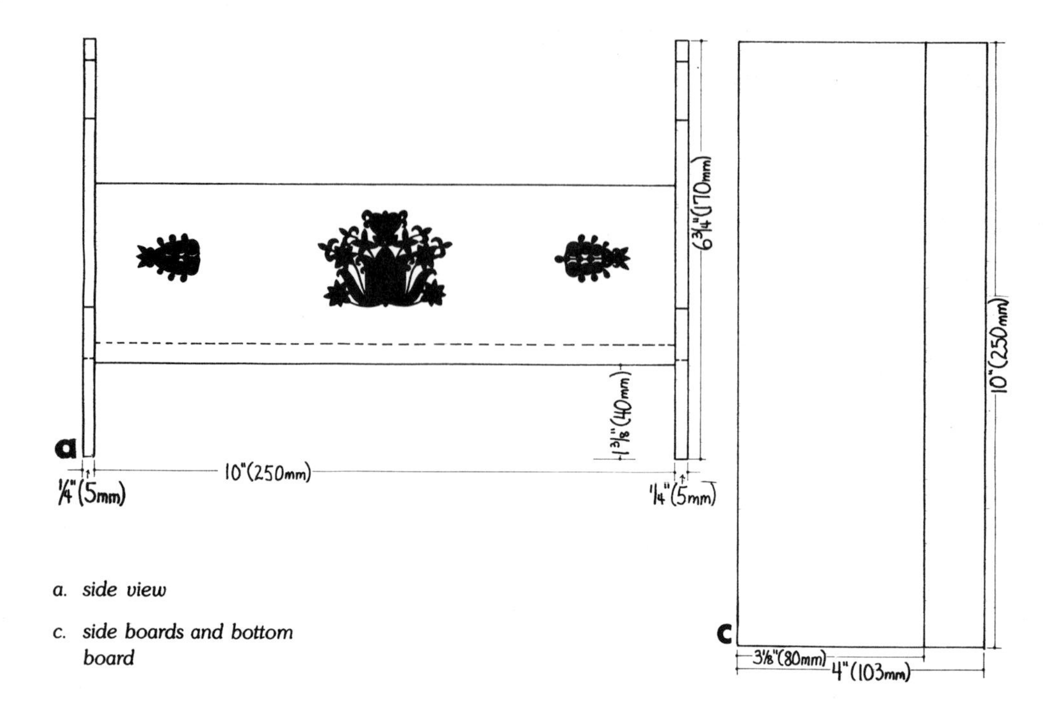

a. *side view*

c. *side boards and bottom board*

To ensure that the end panels (**b**) are exactly the same shape, make a cardboard template and trace around it to transfer the pattern onto the wood.

Use a coping saw to cut out the plywood pieces, then clamp them together so you can sand the edges at the same time. The side panels and the bottom piece (**c**) can be cut out with a circular saw. Sand all of the edges before assembly.

In addition to glue, use small wood screws to fasten the side panels to the bottom piece and to attach the end panels. Drill small holes at pre-marked places to guide the screws in. Countersink the screw heads below the surface of the wood and use spackle (wood filler) to conceal them. Sand smooth when the spackle dries. Using screws gives a

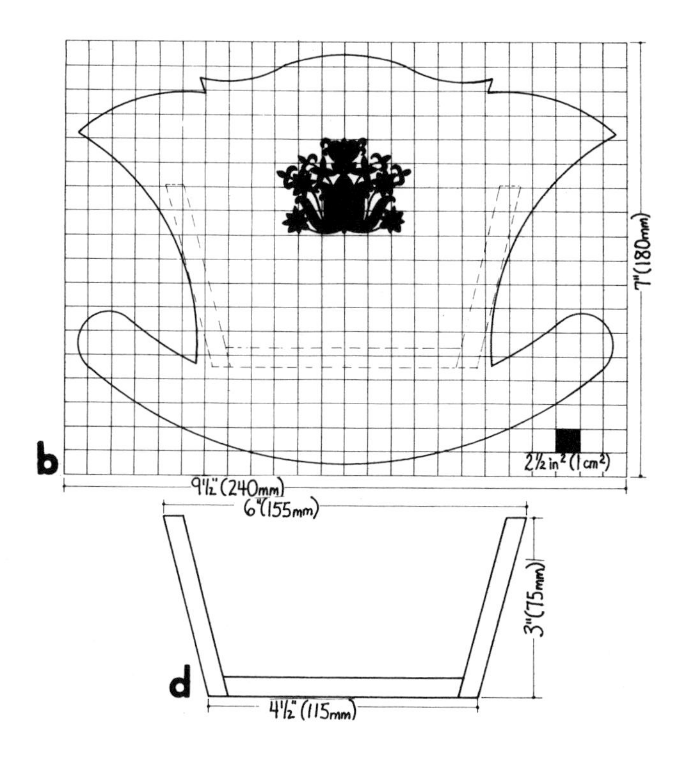

b. front view end panel

d. front view side panels attached to bottom piece

sturdier construction and also eliminates having to use screw clamps which are usually needed to hold the parts together until the glue sets.

Now prime the surfaces and, after they are dry, apply a base coat of paint. After it dries, sand with fine sandpaper and thoroughly dust off. Then brush on a final coat of enamel. For decoration, use decals.

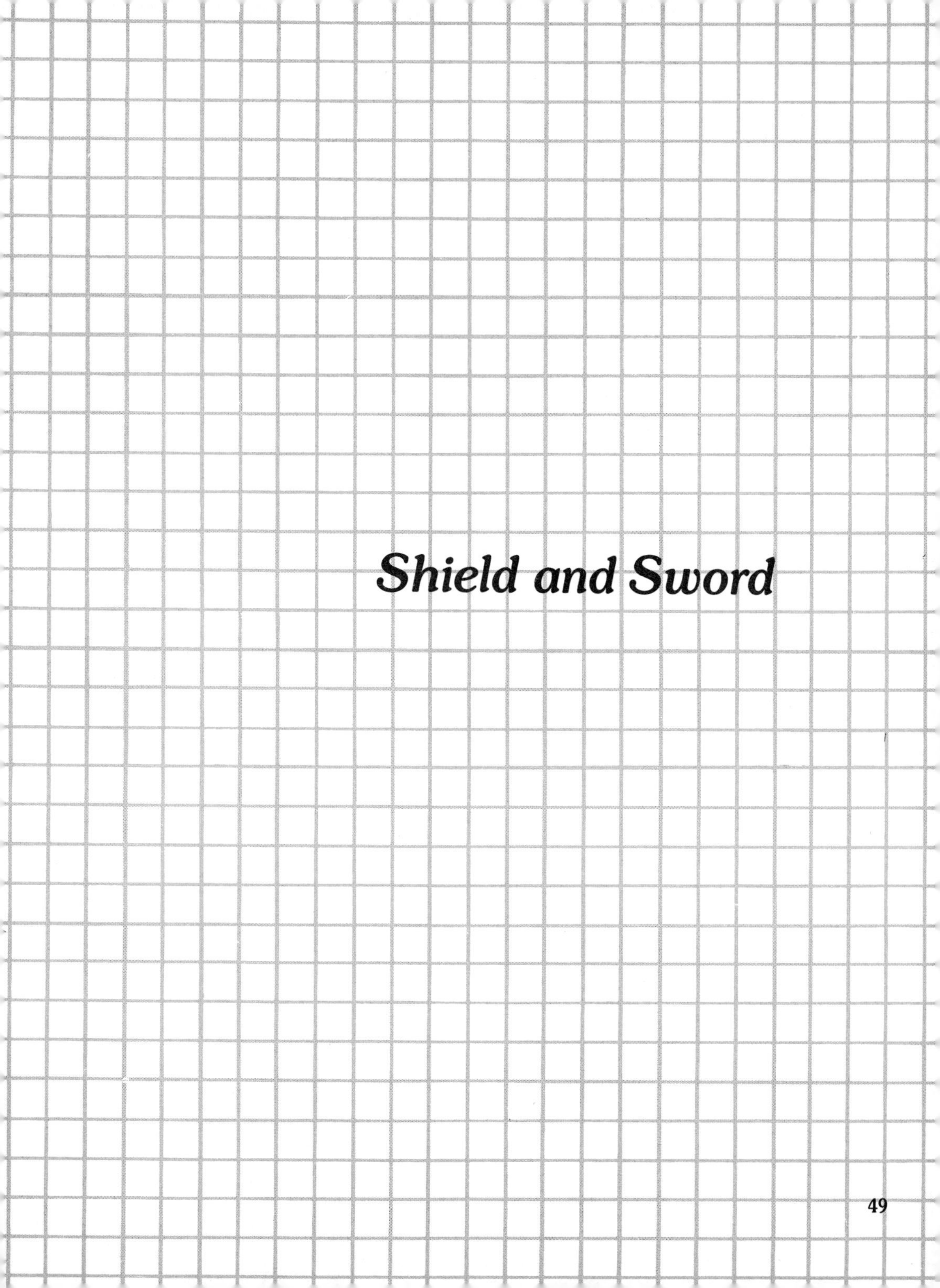

Shield and Sword

Shield and Sword

Beginning with the shield, you will need a piece of $\frac{1}{4}$" (5-mm) -thick plywood, 12 $\frac{1}{2}$" × 15 $\frac{3}{4}$" (320 × 400 mm). Use a coping saw to cut out the shape as indicated on drawing **a**. Cut two $\frac{5}{8}$" (15-mm) firring strips leaving one side straight, rounding the other side as shown in the top view of the finished shield (**c**). Since the shield will receive a fair

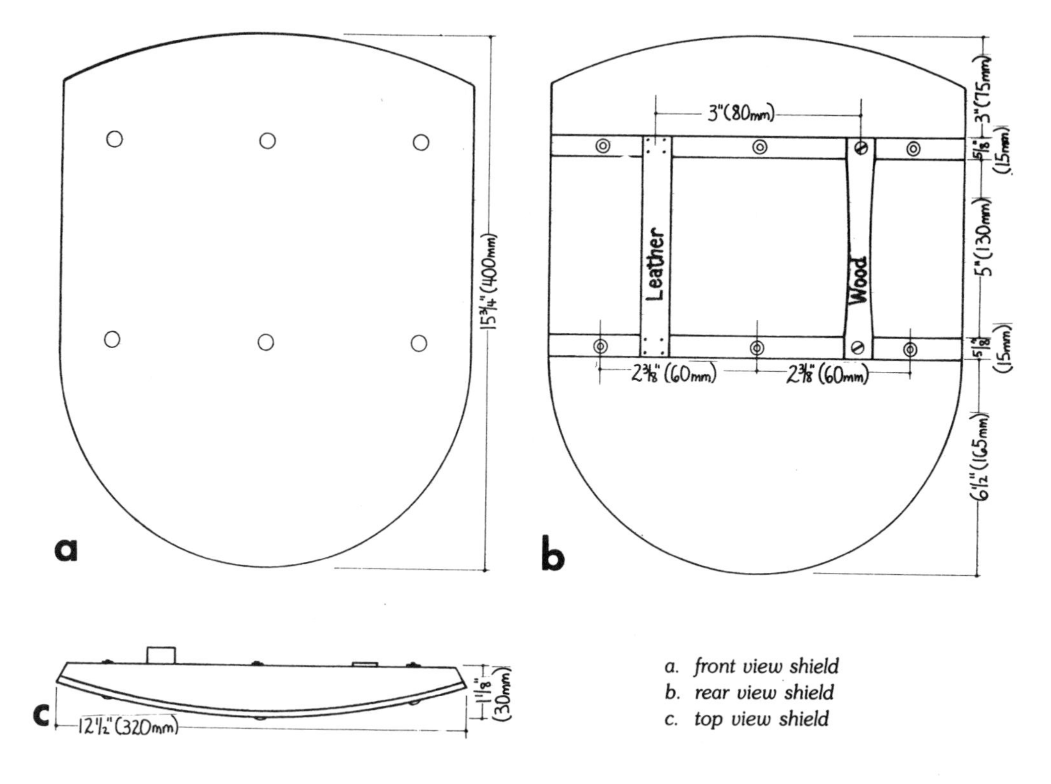

a. front view shield
b. rear view shield
c. top view shield

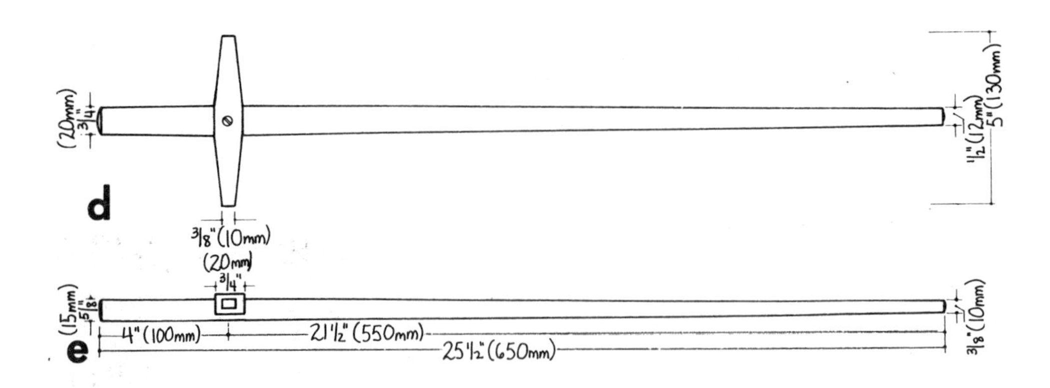

d. top view sword
e. side view sword

amount of stress in "battle," glueing the strips isn't likely to be a strong enough bond. If you have a rivet machine, the rivet heads make an appropriate decoration. Alternatively, use round-head wood screws to create a similar effect. This construction can withstand strong blows.

For ease in handling, attach a leather loop and a wooden handle to the firring strips on the back. The arrangement shown on drawing **b** is for a right-handed person, someone who holds the sword in his right hand and the shield in his left hand. The left arm passes through the leather loop with the hand grasping the wooden handle. For a left-handed person, simply reverse the positions.

The sword is 25 ½" (650 mm) long and made of pine. Follow drawings **d** and **e** to make it. For safety's sake, be sure to leave a very blunt end on the sword.

Both the shield and the sword in the photograph are painted with flat enamel. The shield can also be decorated with decals of heraldic figures and symbols.

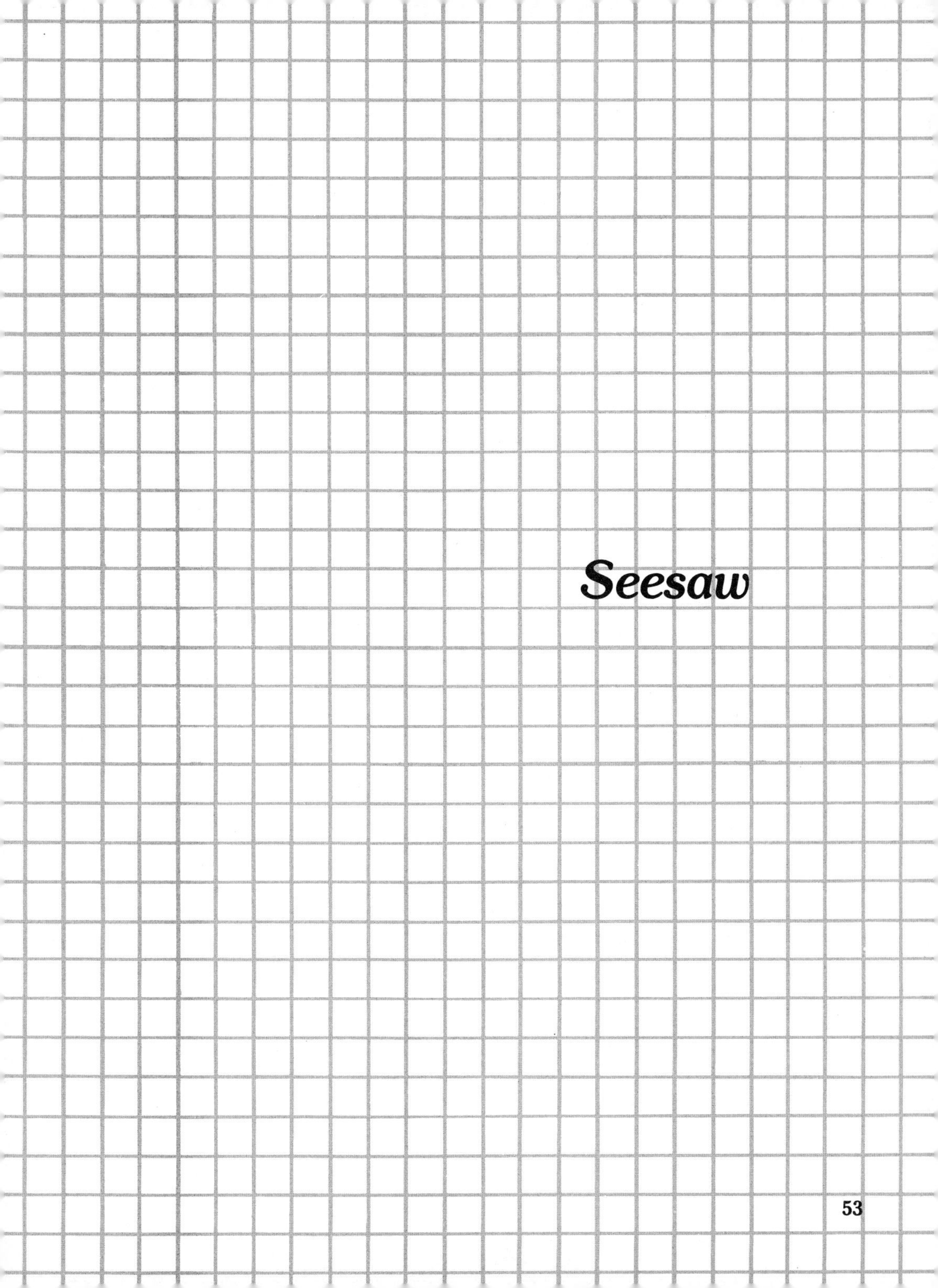

Seesaw

Seesaw

This bowed board is so versatile it not only can be used as a seesaw but also as a deck chair, or, in an upside-down position as a cave, a bridge, or a doll's stage. Two of these units lying on their sides and pushed together become a make-believe boat.

You will need two thin sheets of plywood, $17\frac{1}{2}$″ × 48″ (450 × 1200 mm) not more than $\frac{3}{16}$″ (4 mm) thick glued together.

You will need a temporary holding device for the glueing process. Nail two strong firring strips 39 $\frac{1}{2}$″ (1000 mm) apart on a 20″ (500-mm) -wide board. Bend the first board so that it is held in a curved shape between the two firring strips. Spread the surface with glue. Then place the second board carefully over the first one. Make sure there is a secure and continuous join between the two boards.

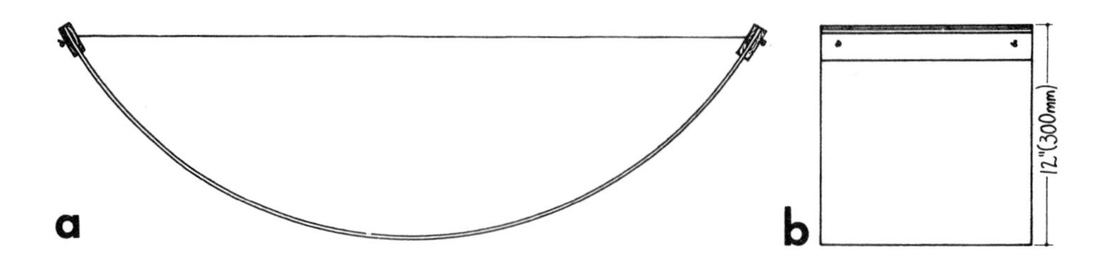

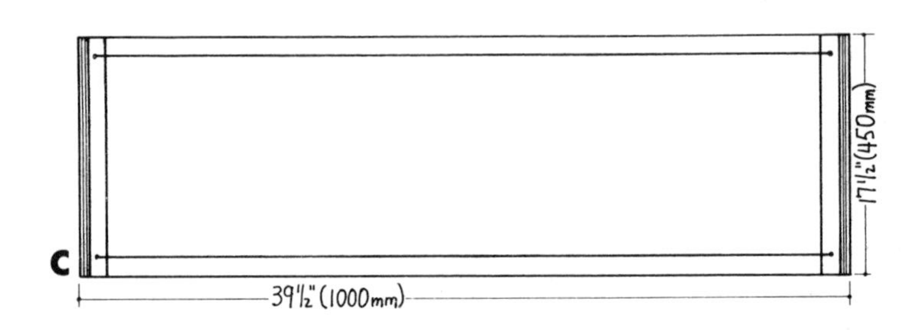

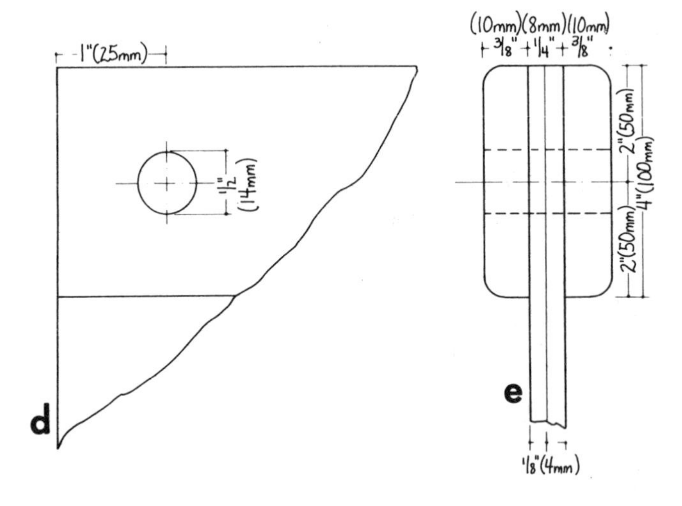

a. side view

b. front view

c. top view

d. detail of size of holes for rope

e. detail of size of firring strips

If necessary, use small screw clamps and wood blocks to hold the pieces together until thoroughly dry. While the glue is setting, prepare four wood strips as shown in profile on drawing **e**.

Make the strips from pine $\frac{3}{8}$" (10 mm) thick and 4" (100 mm) wide. With a router, round the edges with a quarter-round cutter. Cut the 17 $\frac{1}{2}$" (450-mm) -wide ends of the curved boards flush and glue on the end strips. Drill 1 $\frac{1}{2}$" (14-mm) -wide holes through the end strips on a diameter 1" (25 mm) away from the edges at each end (**d**). Connect the ends of the boards with ropes passed through the holes and secured with knots on the outer side.

Finally, smooth the wood and coat it with clear varnish.

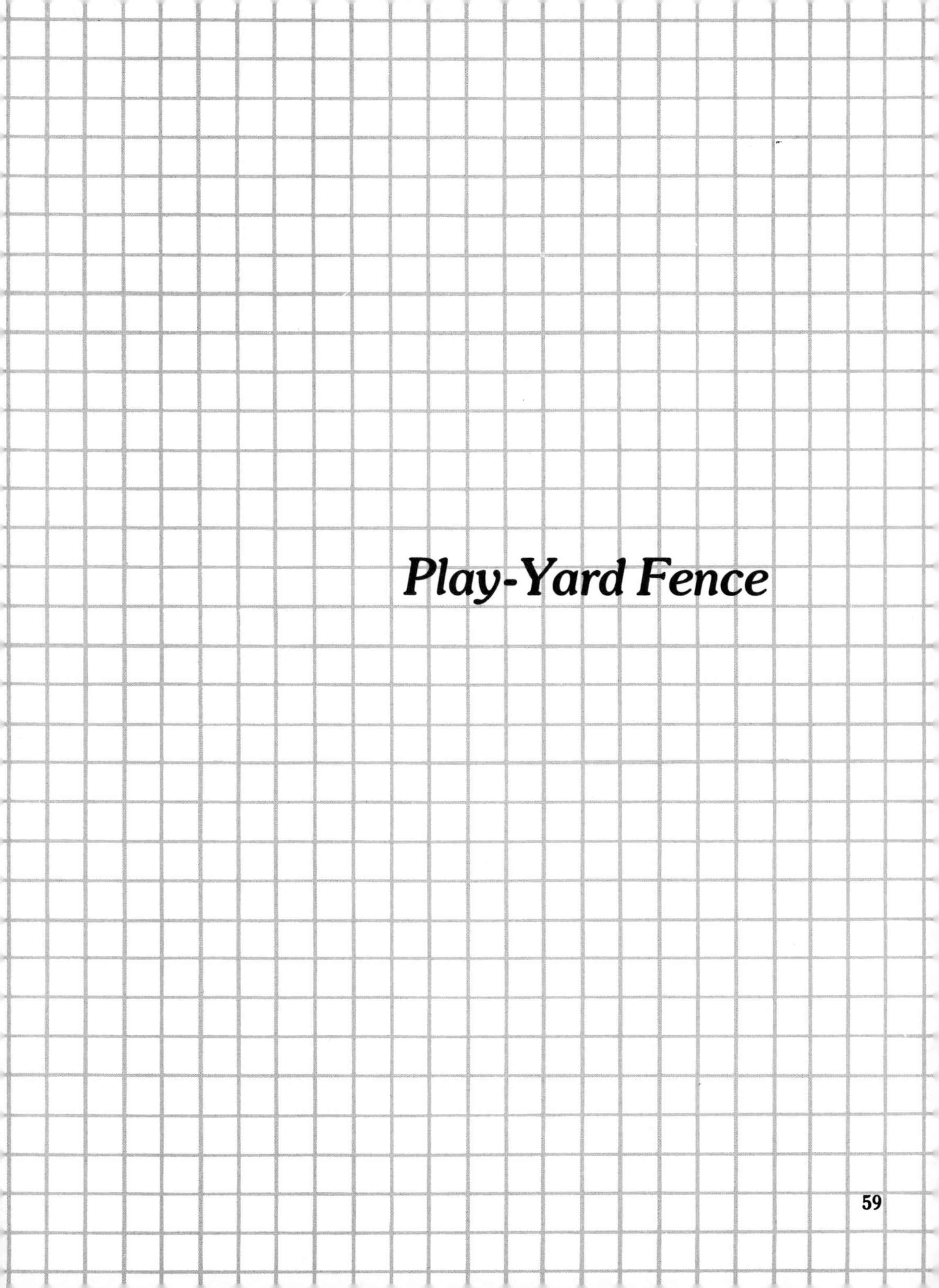

Play-Yard Fence

Play-Yard Fence

The play-yard fence is 6′6″ (200 cm) in diameter. It accommodates at least three young children.

Make the fence from tree trunks or logs, each about 4 ½″ (12 cm) thick. The longest pieces are about 4′6″ (140 cm); the shortest pieces only about 2′6″ (80 cm). See drawing **a**.

You must peel off the rough bark and cut the trunks in varying lengths. The parts above ground have to be well rounded at the top in order to prevent any injuries from sharp edges.

Once the trunks are prepared, coat them thoroughly twice with a water-repellent preservative, allowing them to dry between coats. When they are dry, set-up can begin. Dig a circular trench 6′6″ (200 cm) in diameter, 1′8″ (50 cm) deep, and a spade-width wide. See drawing **c**. Sort the trunks into

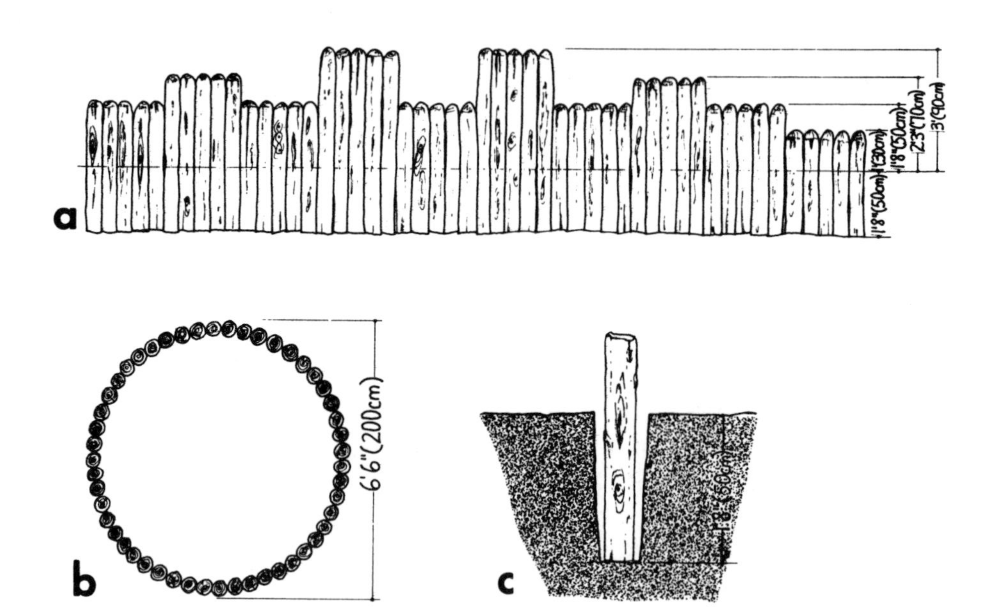

a. arrangement of trunks

b. top view

c. detail of trench

groups by height. Set them into the trench and pour earth in, making sure it is packed down firmly.

To prevent the wood fence from being shifted by active children, place a wire around the outside about 4" (10 cm) above the ground, and staple onto each piece of wood.

Pour sand into the play yard. The sand will fill up the cracks between the trunks. Leave a bare patch of ground around the outside of the play yard so that dropped toys are easy to find.

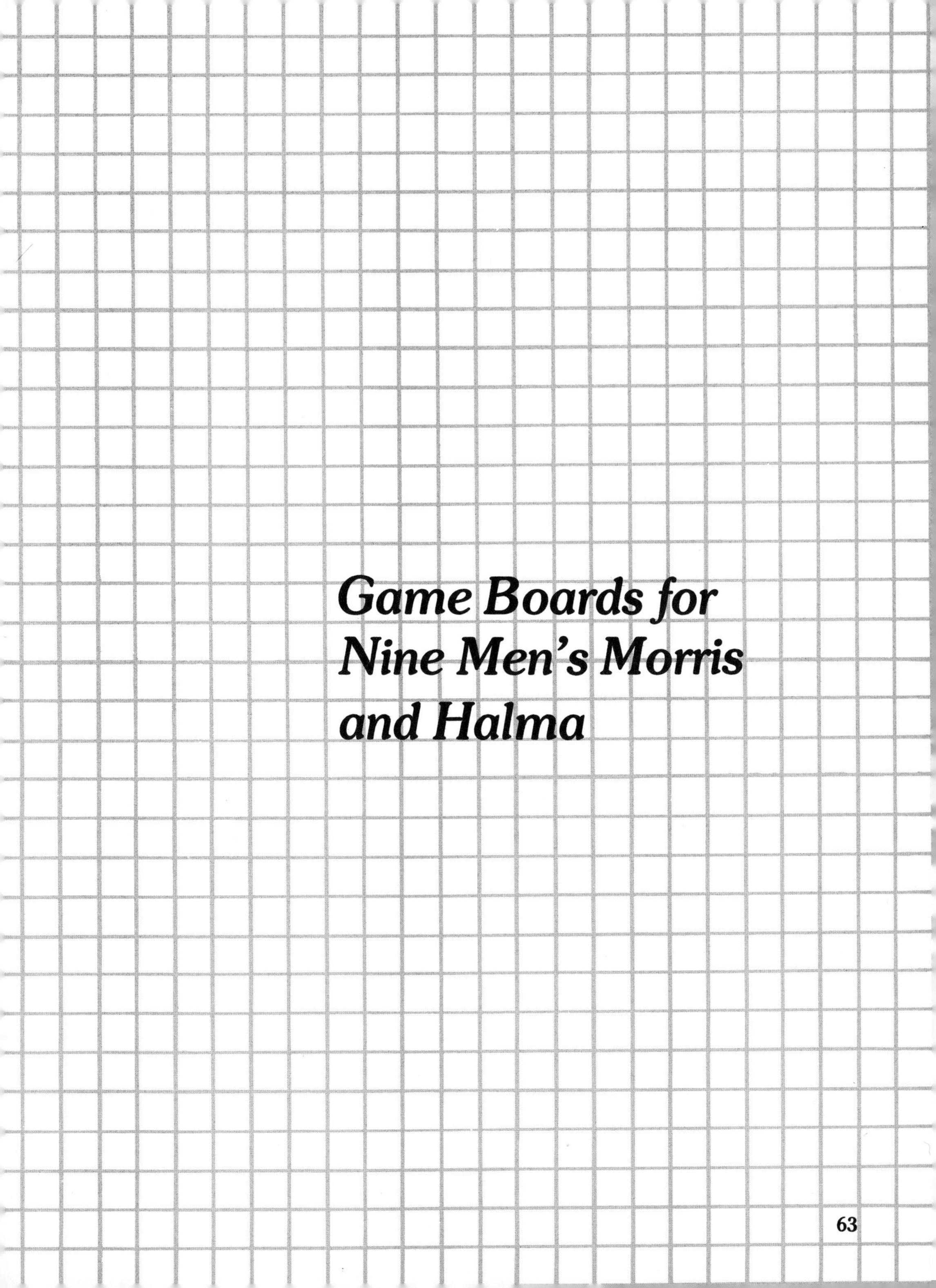

Game Boards for Nine Men's Morris and Halma

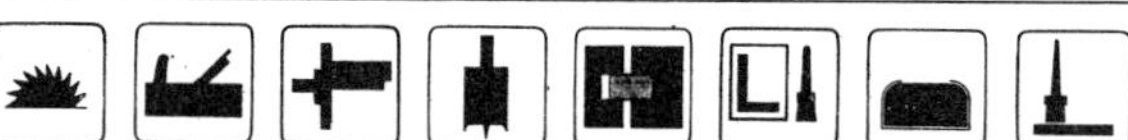

Game Boards for Nine Men's Morris and Halma

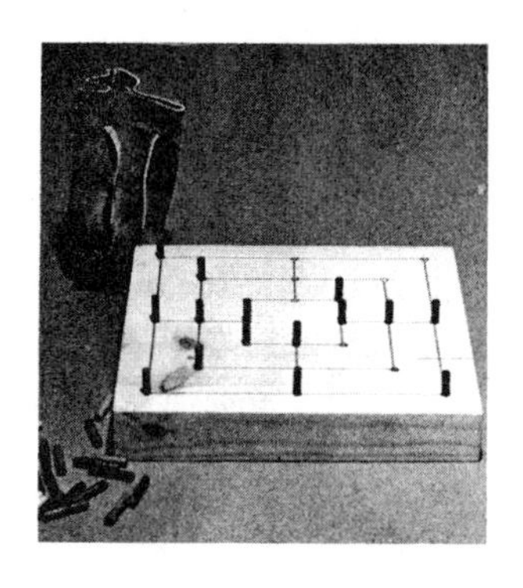

Make the game boards for Halma (**a**) and Nine Men's Morris (**c**) from 1 $\frac{3}{8}$" (35-mm) -thick pieces of pine. Each game board is 8 $\frac{1}{2}$" (220 mm) square. If you need to join two narrower pieces together, use $\frac{3}{8}$" (10 mm) dowels as well as glue to reinforce the joint.

Mark the dowel holes on the edge of one board and lightly hammer in small nails. Snip off the nail heads, then press the side against the corresponding edge of the second board. The nails will leave indentations in the exact spots where the dowels will be inserted. Pull out the marking nails, and drill 1 $\frac{1}{2}$" (40-mm) -deep holes in both boards with a $\frac{7}{16}$" (10-mm) -diameter wood spiral drill.

Now cut 2 $\frac{7}{8}$" (77-mm) -long pieces from a round $\frac{3}{8}$" dowel. Sand the cut edges, and, after appying glue, push the dowels into the holes of one board. Then apply glue to the two surfaces being joined, and press the dowels into the second board, holding everything together lightly with screw clamps. When everything is dry, sand all the edges and flat surfaces.

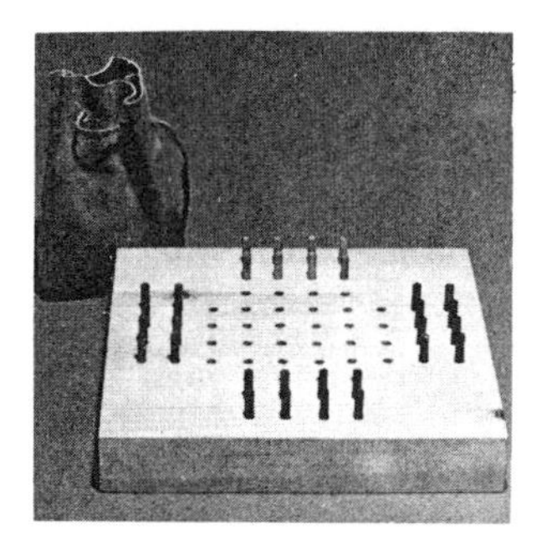

Now drill the holes to hold the game pegs (see drawings **a** and **c**). Mark the centers where shown, and then drill $\frac{3}{8}$" (10-mm) holes (drawings **b** and **d**) with a $\frac{1}{4}$" (6-mm) -diameter wood spiral drill. The

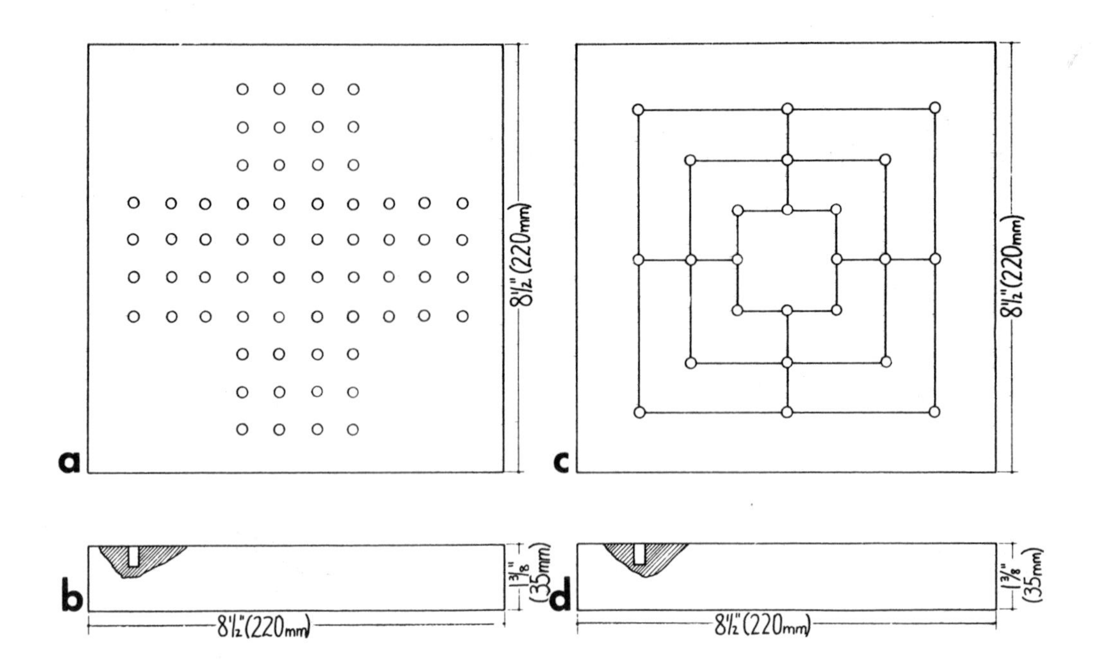

a. top view Halma board

b. side view Halma board

c. top view Morris board

d. side view Halma board

game pegs must be thinner than the holes; therefore, use $\frac{3}{16}$" (5-mm) dowels. Cut off 1" (25-mm) pieces. Sand the ends smooth so they will slide easily into the holes as you play.

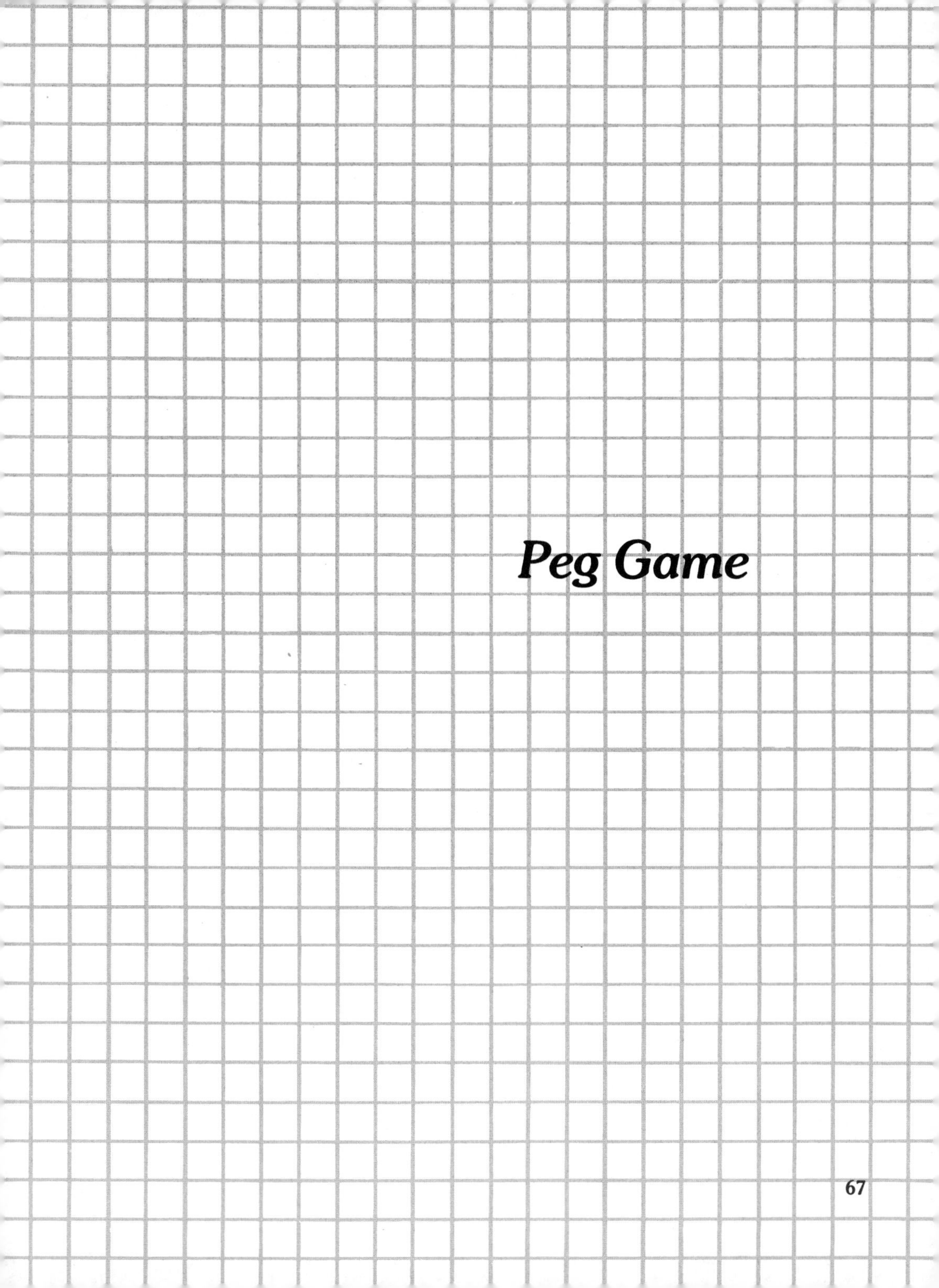

Peg Game

Peg Game

This peg game is for two players. The rules are as follows: Each player has 12 game pegs and they take turns moving. A player can move one hole at a time in a straight or diagonal line, as well as jump over his own or his enemy's peg if there is a free hole immediately beyond it. No backwards movement is allowed.

Each player's goal is to move all of his pegs to the far side of the board first with all the pegs in the opposite starting position. If it comes to a blockade, the player who can't move loses.

Make the game board out of 1 ⅝″ (40-mm) pine, cut to 5″ (125 mm) wide by 13″ (325 mm) long. Smooth the surfaces and long sides with a fine plane, working always in the direction of the grain. Sand the short ends of the board with a sanding block or with a sanding disk attached to your drill. Planing against the grain is difficult even for a professional woodworker.

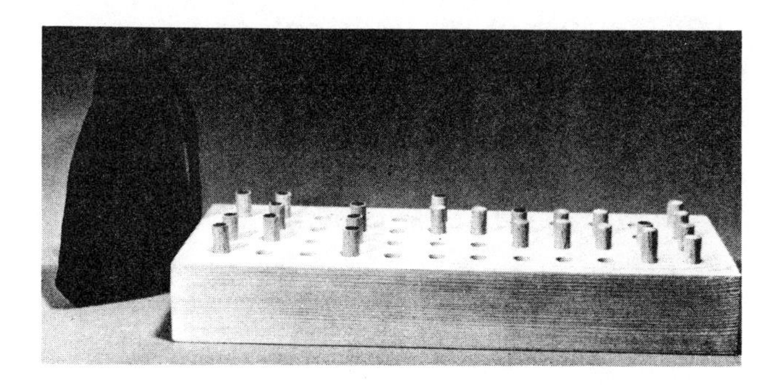

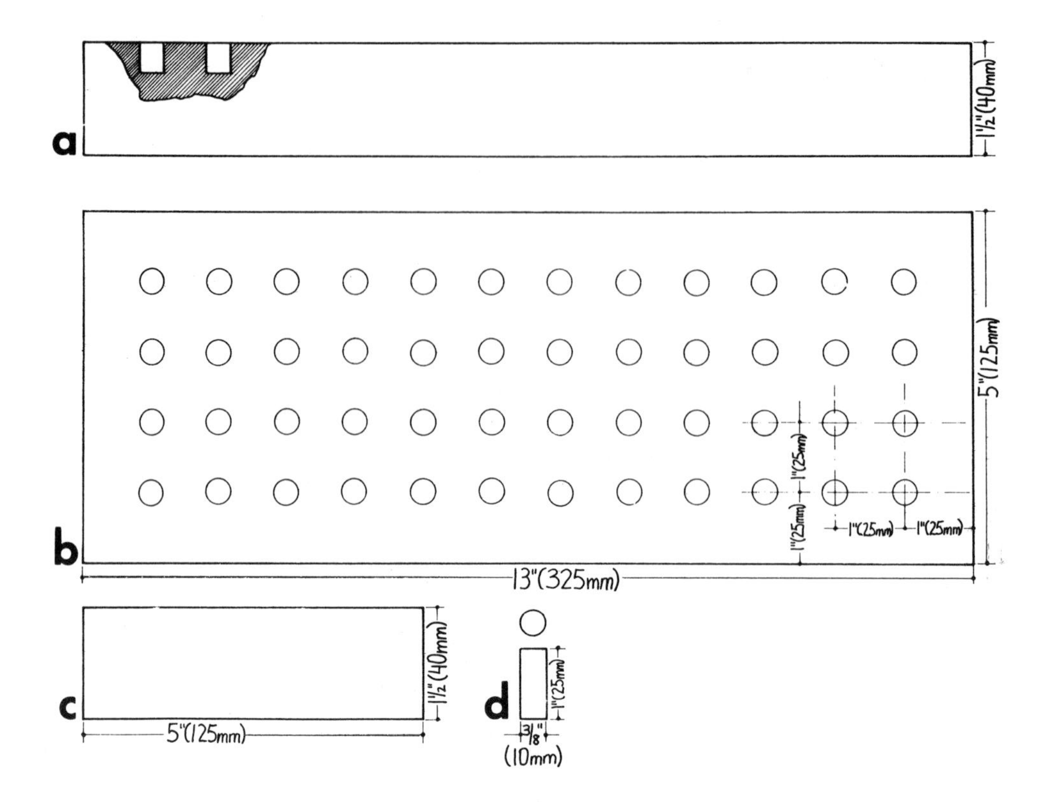

a. side view

b. top view

c. short side

d. game pegs

Drill 3/8" (10-mm) holes with a 7/16" (10-mm) -diameter wood spiral bit at the points as shown on drawing **b.**

Now make the 24 game pegs (**d**) from 3/8" (10-mm) -diameter wood dowels. Use a fine-tooth saw. Use fine sandpaper to smooth out any cutting marks.

Stain or paint 12 of the pegs and leave the other 12 natural, or paint them in a different color. Coat the board itself with clear varnish.

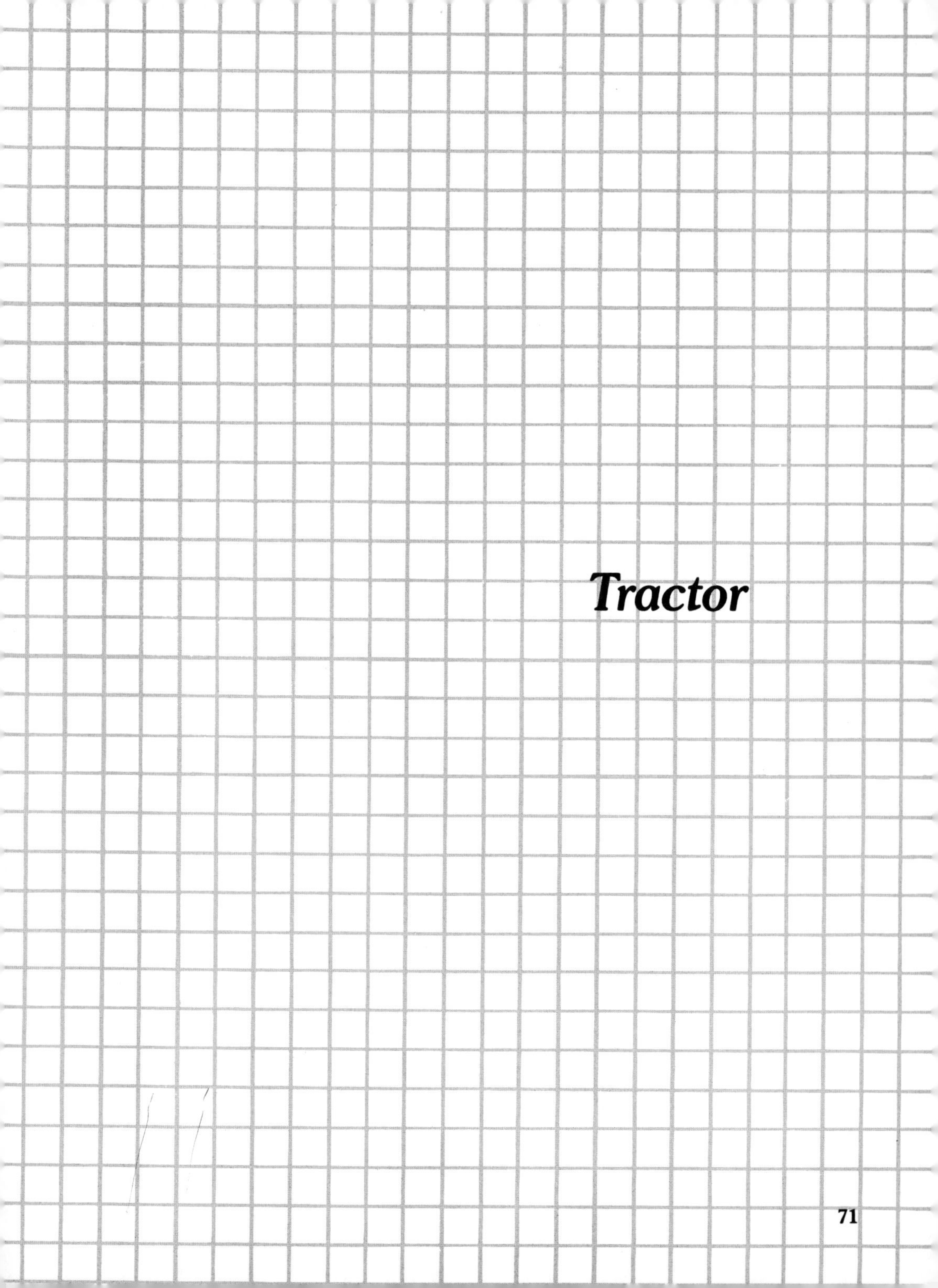

Tractor

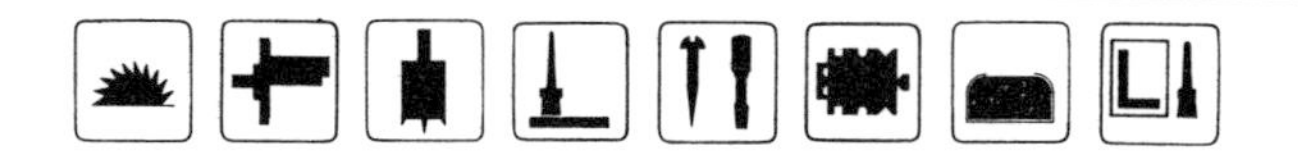

Tractor

This tractor is made of pine except for the wheels, muffler and the muffler base.

Start by cutting out the chassis (**d**). Then the rear axle (**o**) and the two half-round mounts (**l**) for the front swing axle are glued onto the chassis. Also cut out the front swing axle (**k**).

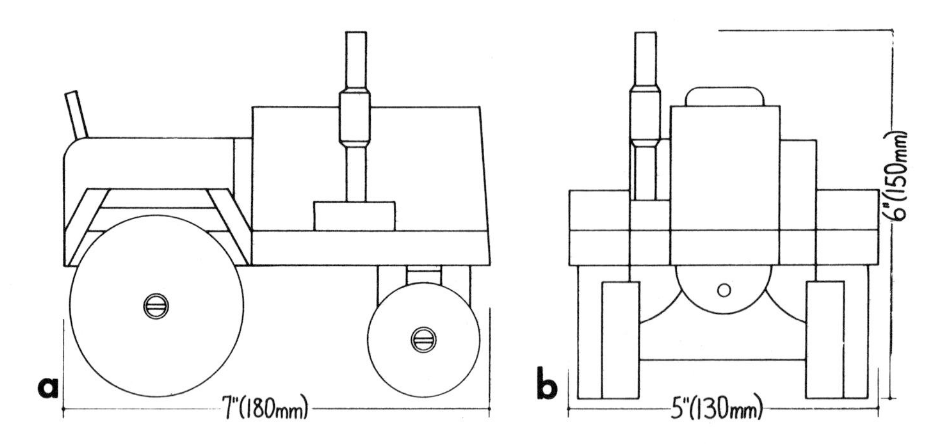

a. side view

b. front view

While the glue is drying, you can work on the parts that have to be turned. Start with the wheels (**i**, **j**). When finished, attach them with metal screws. The front swing axle is connected to its mounts (**l**) by a metal pin. A driving test over rough ground will show how the swing axle works.

Next, make the engine (**e**) and the driver's seat enclosure (**f**). Both are glued on.

Now prepare the fenders (**g**). Make certain that

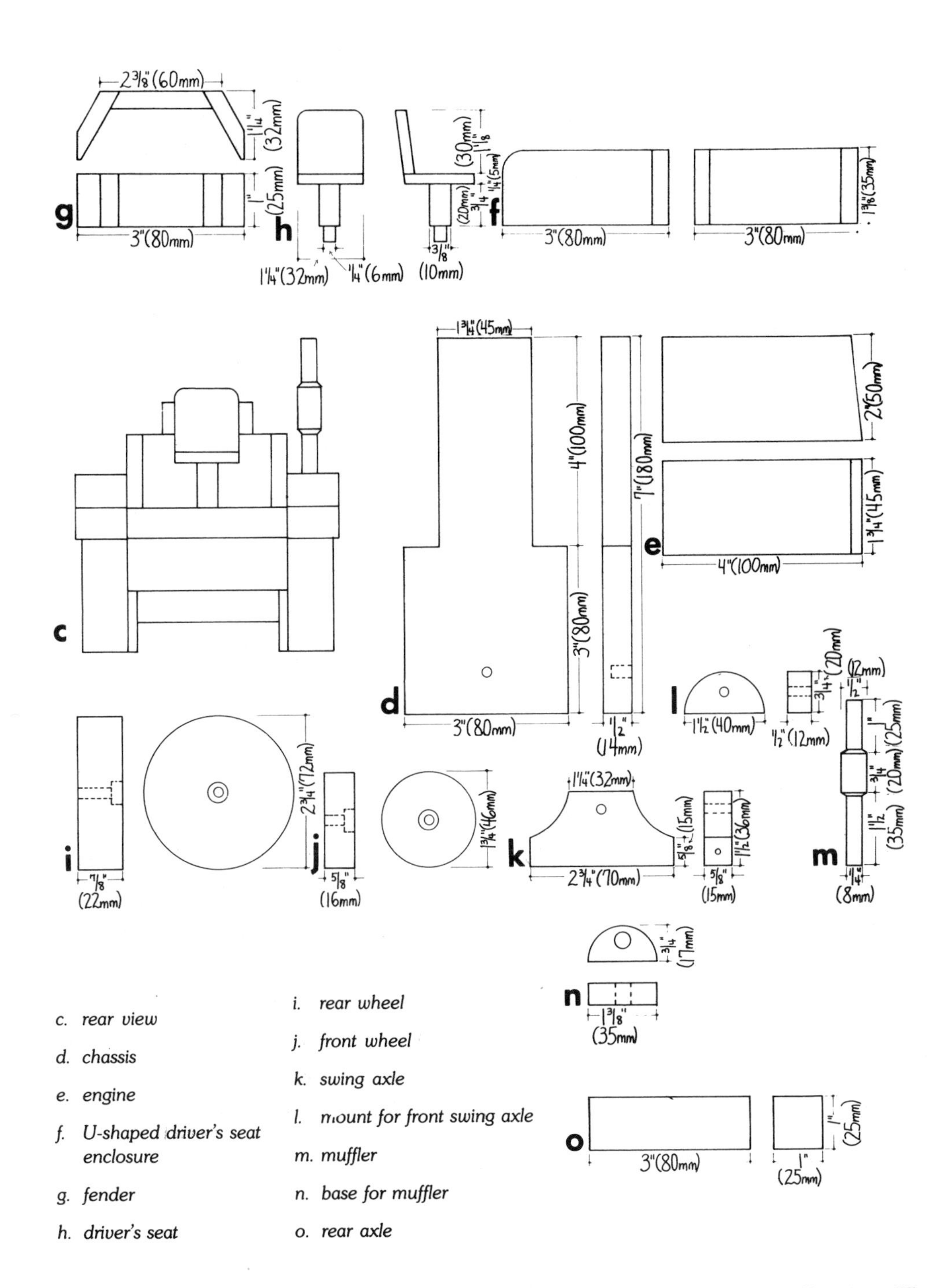

c. rear view

d. chassis

e. engine

f. U-shaped driver's seat enclosure

g. fender

h. driver's seat

i. rear wheel

j. front wheel

k. swing axle

l. mount for front swing axle

m. muffler

n. base for muffler

o. rear axle

the driver's seat enclosure is flush with the chassis. If it isn't, sand it down before glueing the fenders on.

After turning, glue the muffler (**m**) into the half-round base (**n**). Glue these parts onto the right side of the engine block.

Now make the driver's seat (**h**). You need two small, $\frac{1}{4}$" (5-mm) -thick boards, one for the back and one for the seat, plus one round piece $\frac{3}{8}$" (10 mm) at one end, $\frac{1}{4}$" (6 mm) at the other. Glue the large end onto the seat bottom. The other end is stuck into the floor of the chassis but not glued, so that it can swivel like the real thing. You can turn this piece or start with a $\frac{3}{8}$" dowel, filing and sanding down the one end.

To make the trailer and the burlap bags shown in the photograph, see pages 79 and 88.

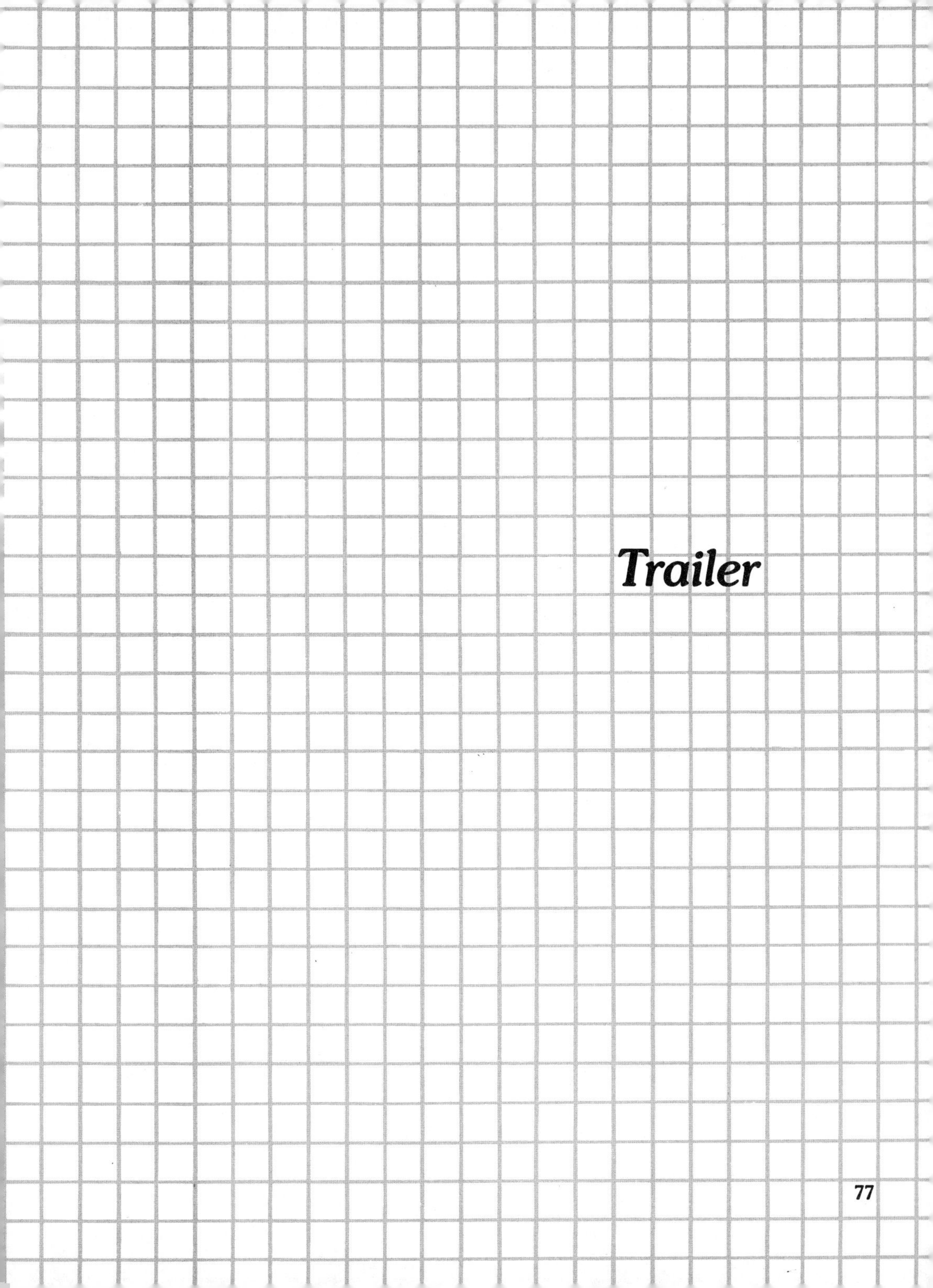

Trailer

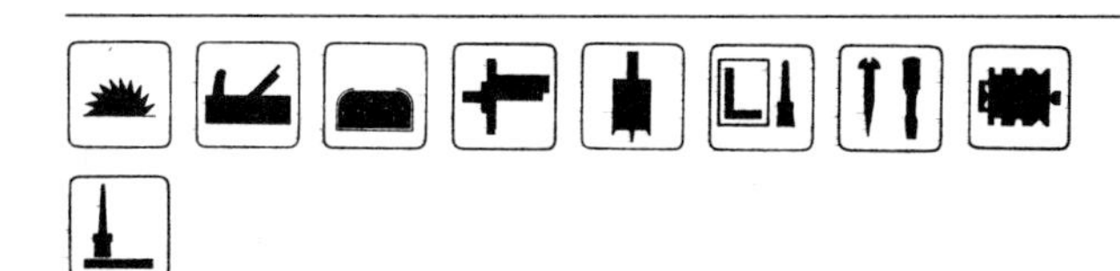

Trailer

This trailer is made to be used with the tractor on page 73.

The side and end panels are $\frac{1}{4}''$ (6 mm) thick. You can do all straight cuts with a circular saw; therefore, you must use a marking gauge in order to ensure parallel cuts. Smooth the sawed edges. Connect the side panels and the end panels with glue and, when the glue is dry, add the bottom piece. Sand all outer edges.

Now cut out the axles (**e**, **f**). They are the same size but their shapes differ slightly. The rear axle (**e**) can be glued on as cut out. The front axle (**f**), however, needs a groove where a round wooden plate (**g**) is glued in. This plate enables the front axle to turn smoothly.

Then screw on the front axle through the bottom part with a wood screw. The screw should be turned in only to the point where the axle can still turn easily.

After the wheels (**h**) are turned on the lathe, they are ready to be mounted.

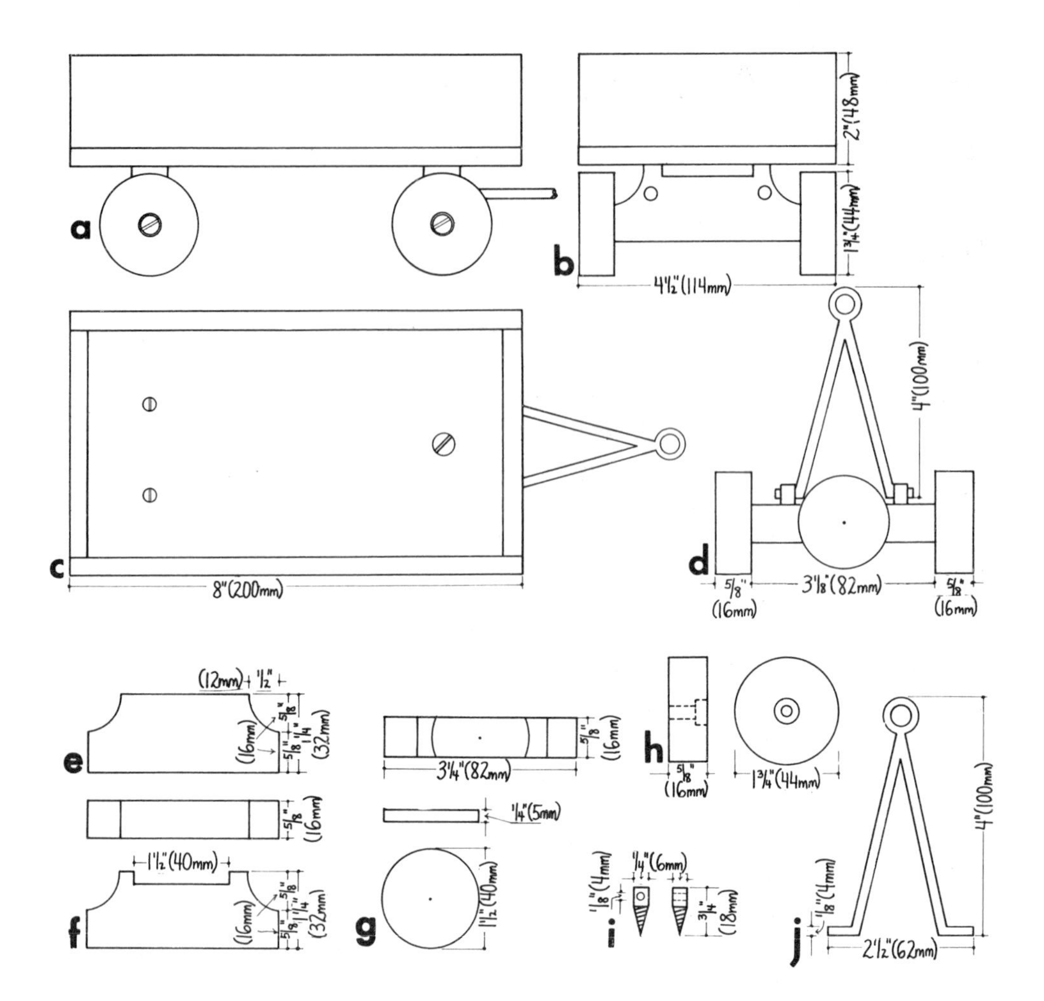

a. side view
b. front view without trailer hitch
c. top view
d. detail of turning axle
e. rear axle
f. front axle
g. turn of front axle
h. wheel
i. screw loops for trailer hitch
j. trailer hitch

Finally, make the V-shaped hitch (**j**) out of a 1″ (4 mm) metal rod, and solder a ring onto the front end. Make the attachments for the shaft ends that are connected to the front axle (**d**) from two $\frac{1}{4}$″ (6-mm)-thick metal screws. Cut off the heads and drill $\frac{1}{8}$″ (4-mm)-wide holes through the tops of the screw shanks (**i**). These parts can be screwed into the wood easily if you pre-drill the holes and then use a nail stuck through the loops to turn the screws until they are tight.

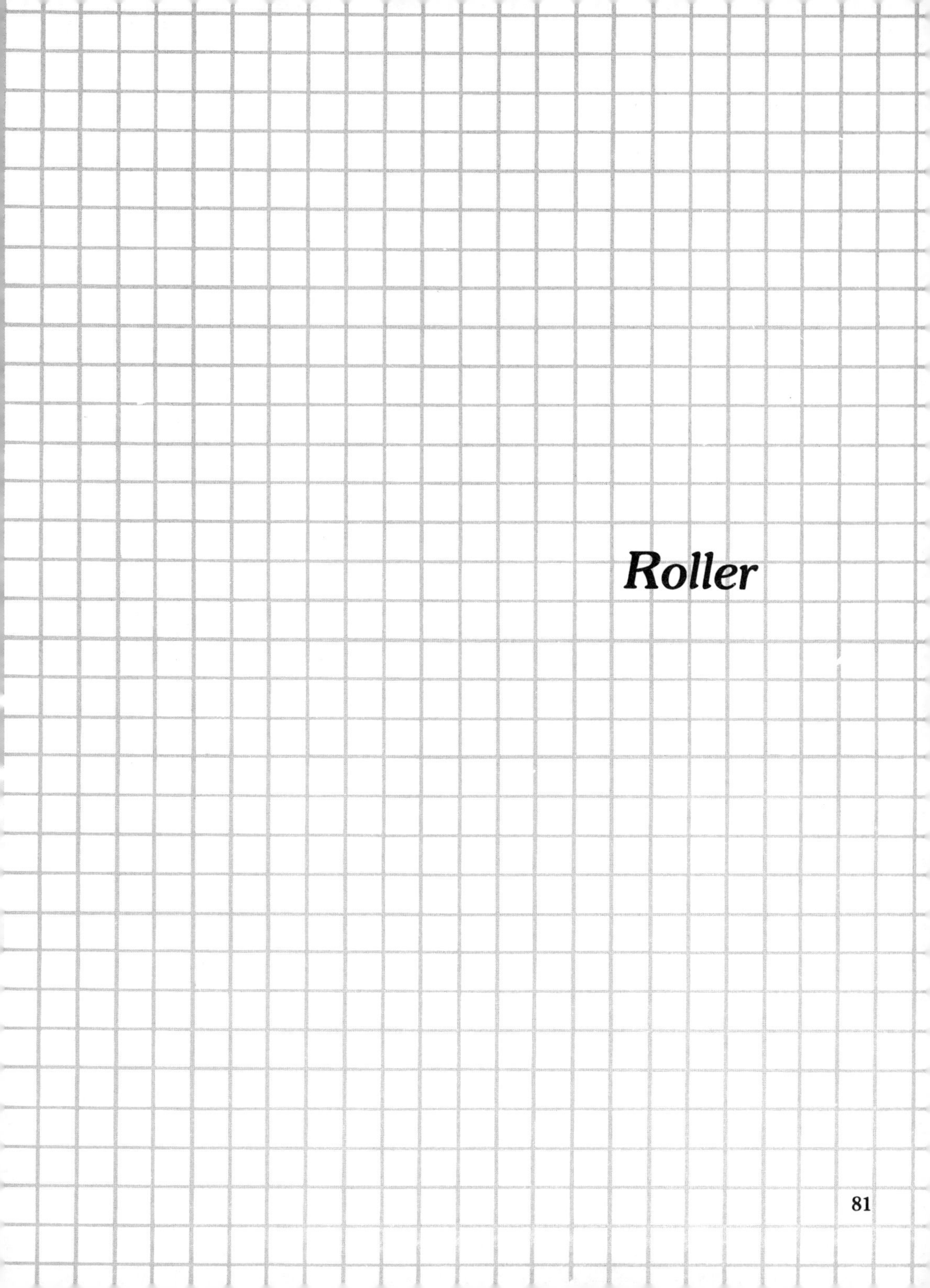

Roller

  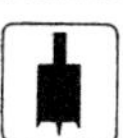  

Roller

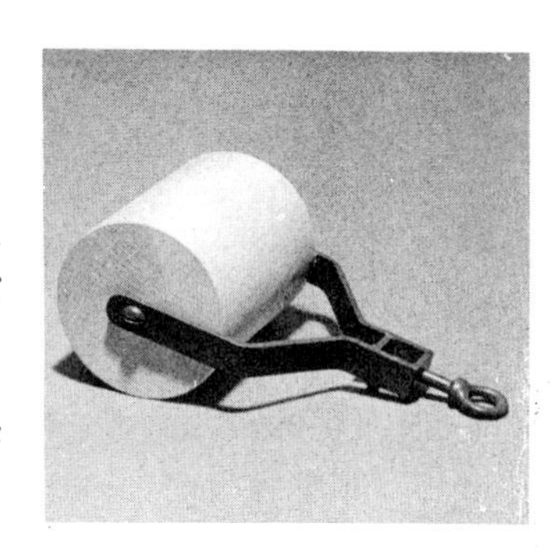

The roller is for use with the tractor on page 73. The only wooden part is the cylinder (**c**). This can either be turned from one piece of thick wood or from several pieces glued together.

Making the metal pulling fork **e** involves the use of a vise, a file, a soldering iron and a drill—all of which you should have in your home workshop. The hauling fork is made of flat metal $\frac{1}{8}$" (3 mm) thick and $\frac{5}{8}$" (15 mm) wide.

Shape the two side pieces by tightening the metal strip in a vise and making two 45° bends. Cut two $\frac{1}{2}$" (14-mm) -long pieces of metal and drill a $\frac{5}{16}$" (6.6-mm) hole in the middle of each. File the ends perfectly flat, then solder the two pieces between

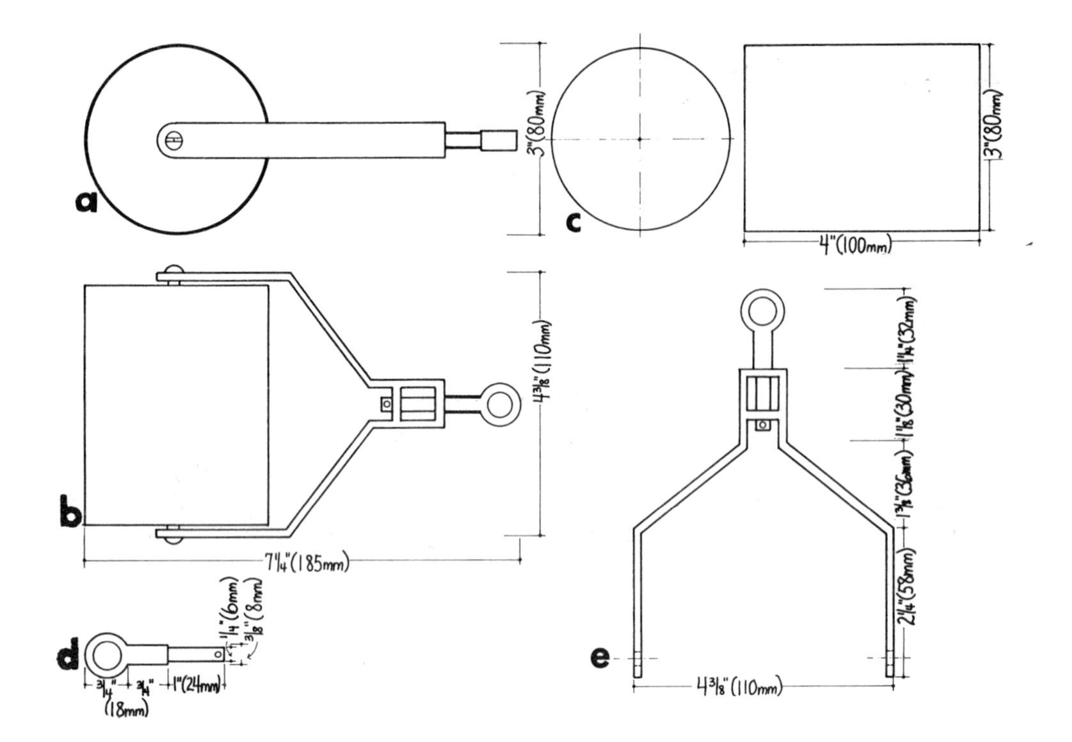

a. side view

b. top view

c. wood roller

d. metal hitch

e. metal pulling fork with turnable hitch

the angled edge pieces as shown in drawing **e**. Drill $\frac{5}{16}$″ (6.6-mm) holes in the wide ends of the hauling fork. The round wood roller can now be attached by round-head screws passed through the holes in the end of the fork. Be sure to use screws slightly smaller than the holes so the roller will turn easily.

Next you need to make the hitch itself. You may have an eye hook that is just the right size. Alternatively you can cut a piece of $\frac{1}{4}$″ (6 mm) metal rod and solder a ring on the end of it. Slide the hitch through the holes in the end of the fork and secure it in place by means of a small pin put through a hole in the end. This construction allows the roller some play as it passes over rough ground.

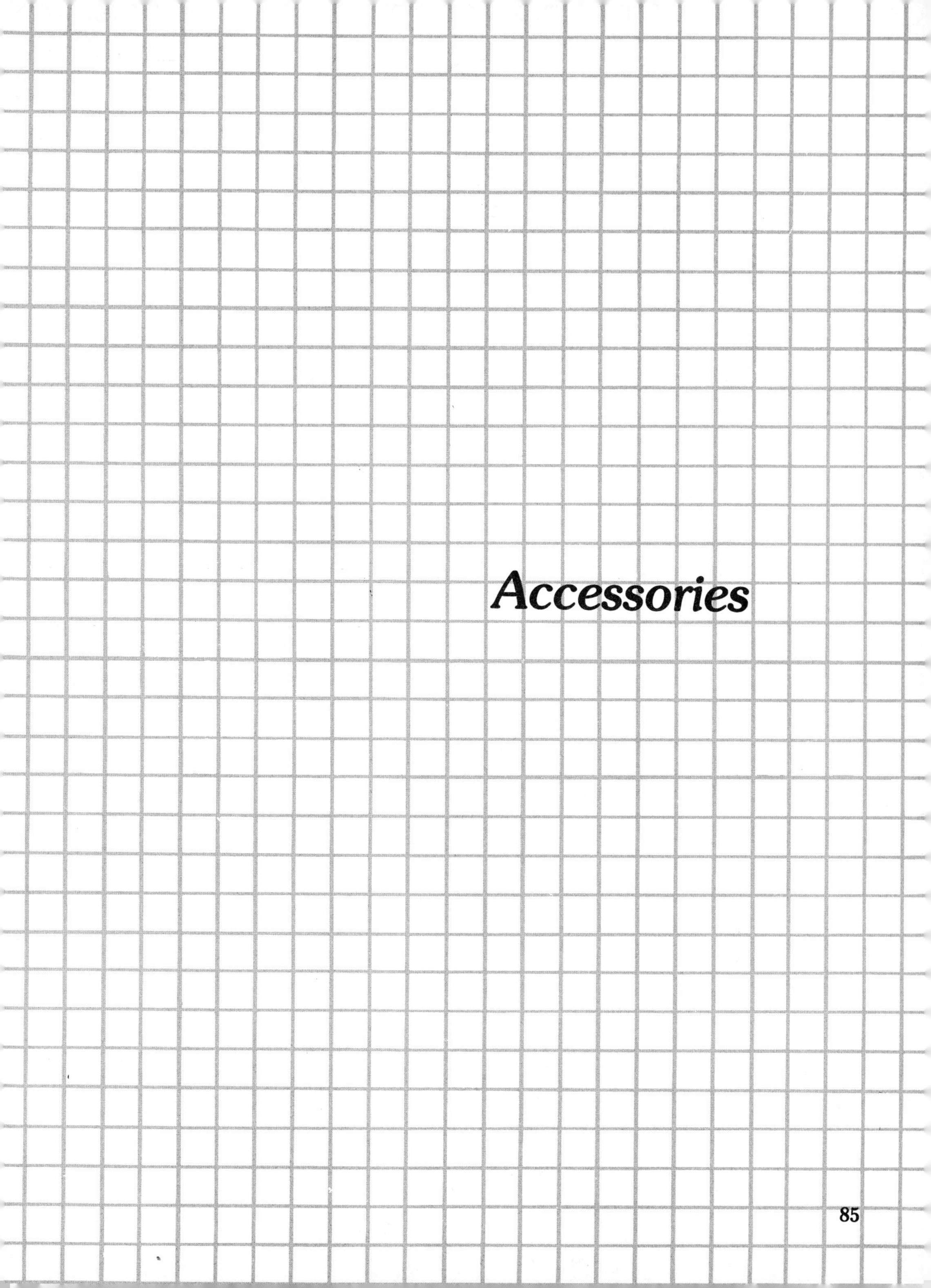

Accessories

Accessories

You can supply the cranes, derricks and trucks described so far with various kinds of accessories for a realistic effect.

For example, you might make buckets **c** which can carry sand for the derrick and the truck crane from $\frac{1}{4}''$ (5-mm) -thick wood and metal wires for handles. Solder a loop on top of the handle (see photo on page 15) for the crane hook.

Drawing **a** shows a cable drum made of two round wooden pieces, 2 $\frac{3}{4}''$ (60 mm) in diameter, fastened together with small, 1 $\frac{1}{2}''$ (40-mm) -long wood strips. In the middle is a hole for the crane hook.

Make the logs (**b**) from branches, sawed into pieces about 2 $\frac{3}{4}''$ (70 mm) long and 1″ (25 mm) in diameter.

The stack of lumber (**d**) consists of rough strips $\frac{3}{8}'' \times \frac{7}{8}''$ (7×22 mm), glued together. Tie a piece of cord around it, leaving a knot on the top so that it can be picked up by the crane hook.

An additional idea is a simple crate (**e**), also made of small strips. The stencil letters on top indicate its destination.

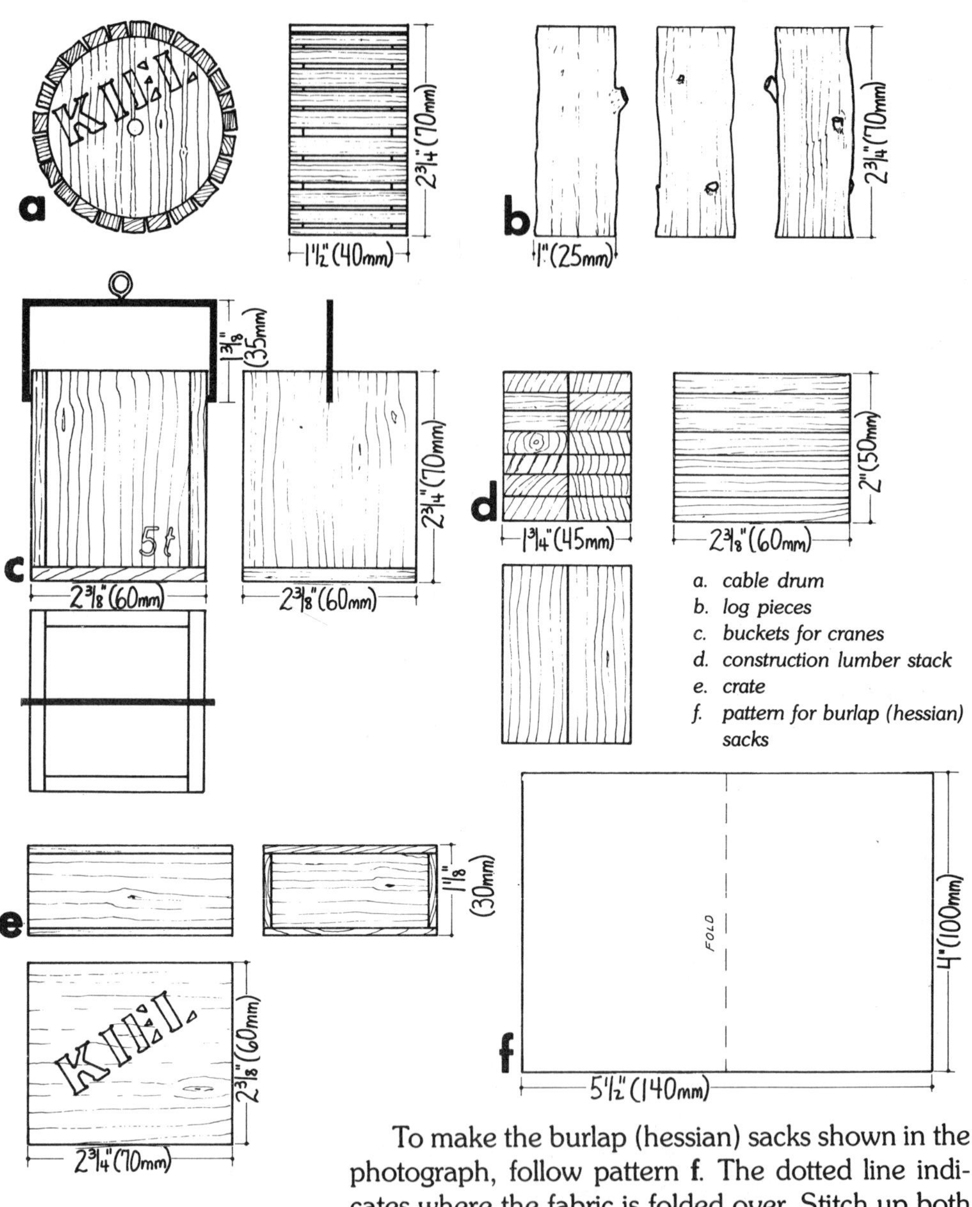

a. *cable drum*
b. *log pieces*
c. *buckets for cranes*
d. *construction lumber stack*
e. *crate*
f. *pattern for burlap (hessian) sacks*

To make the burlap (hessian) sacks shown in the photograph, follow pattern **f**. The dotted line indicates where the fabric is folded over. Stitch up both sides on a sewing machine; then turn the sack inside out. Fill with whatever "produce" you wish and tie the open ends securely with cord.

Cargo Airplane

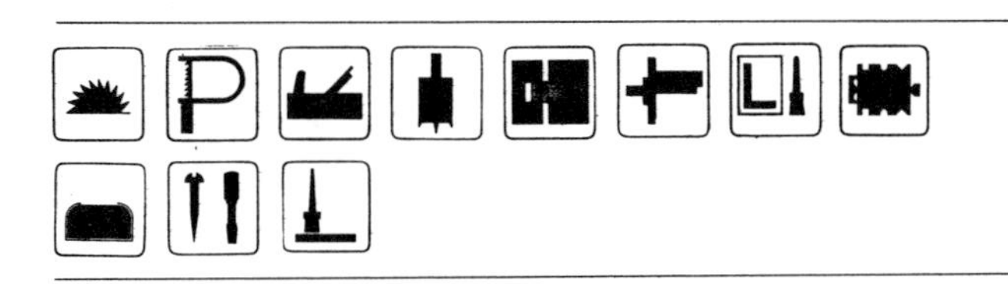

Cargo Airplane

You can tell from the drawings that the work for this project is quite extensive.

Start by constructing the fuselage **c**. The basic parts needed are $\frac{3}{8}$" (10 mm) thick. The top piece of the fuselage is straight. The side and bottom panels narrow towards the tail and form a 1" (25-mm) square at the end, leaving a small open square

a. *side view*

b. *front view*

c. *fuselage*

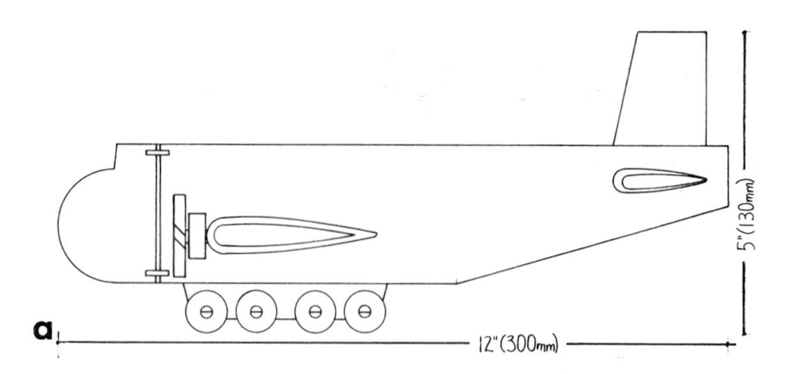

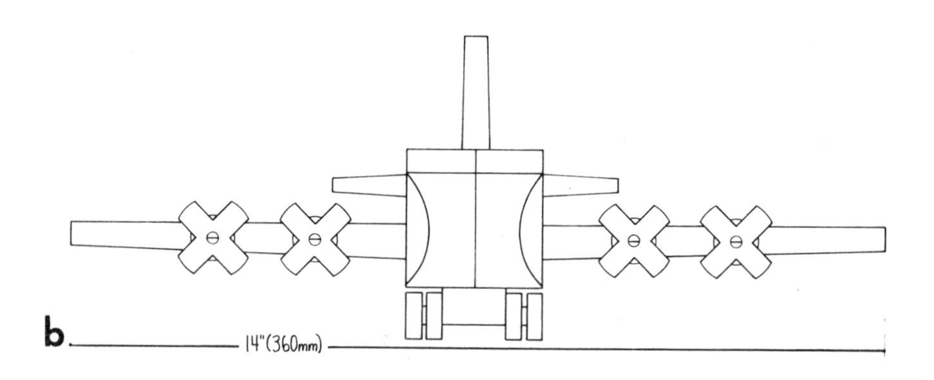

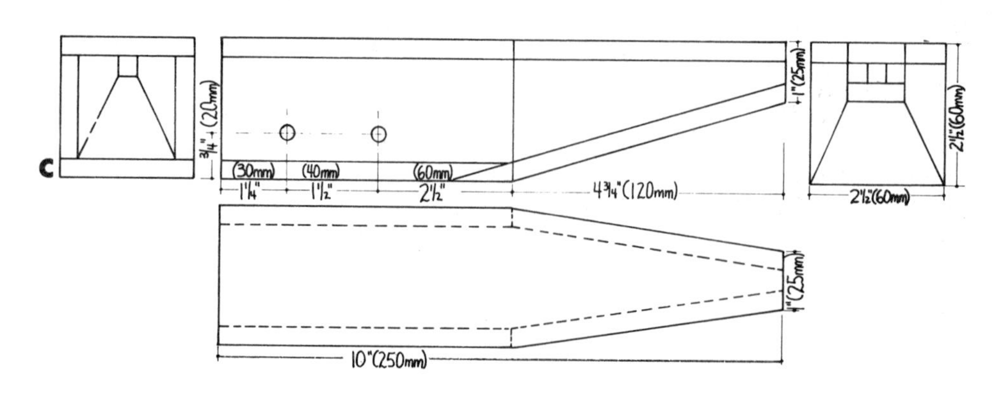

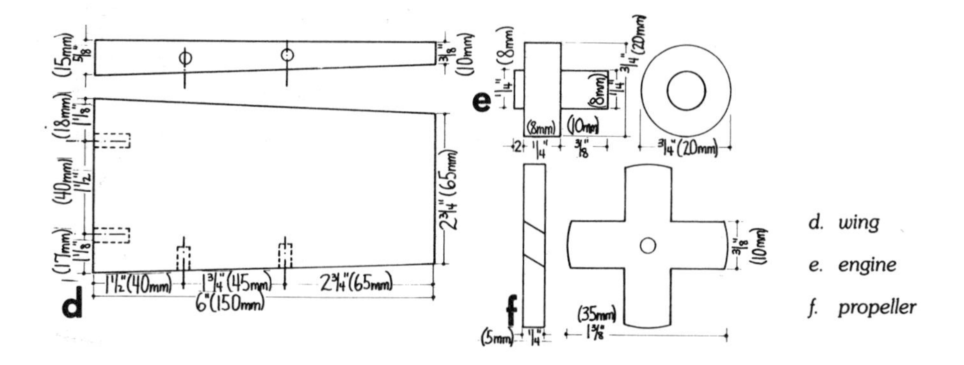

d. *wing*

e. *engine*

f. *propeller*

through which you can poke a stick in order to push out any cargo which may get stuck in the tail.

Make the nose (**g**) from two separate pieces of solid wood, attached by hinges. These open out on either side to give access to the cargo area.

The wings (**d**), the fin (**h**), and the elevators (**i**) are solid wood. Mount the wings on the fuselage with dowels, and glue on the other parts.

The engines (**e**) are made of wood pieces turned on a lathe or from sections of dowel. Then bore $\frac{5}{16}$" (8-mm) -deep holes in the wings (**d**) and glue in the engines.

Cut the plywood propellers (**f**) with a coping saw into the appropriate shape. Shape the blades of the propellers with a file. Attach the finished propellers with screws.

The landing gear (**j**) consists of one wood block. Attached to it are eight twin wheels (**k**) which you must turn on the lathe. Drill $\frac{1}{8}$" (3-mm) holes in the landing gear and also attach the wheels. Be sure to mount the wheels level with each other so that all 16 of them touch the ground when the plane is taxiing.

Fasten the complete landing gear with wheels (**j**) mounted onto the fuselage with glue and four screws. The landing gear is large enough and posi-

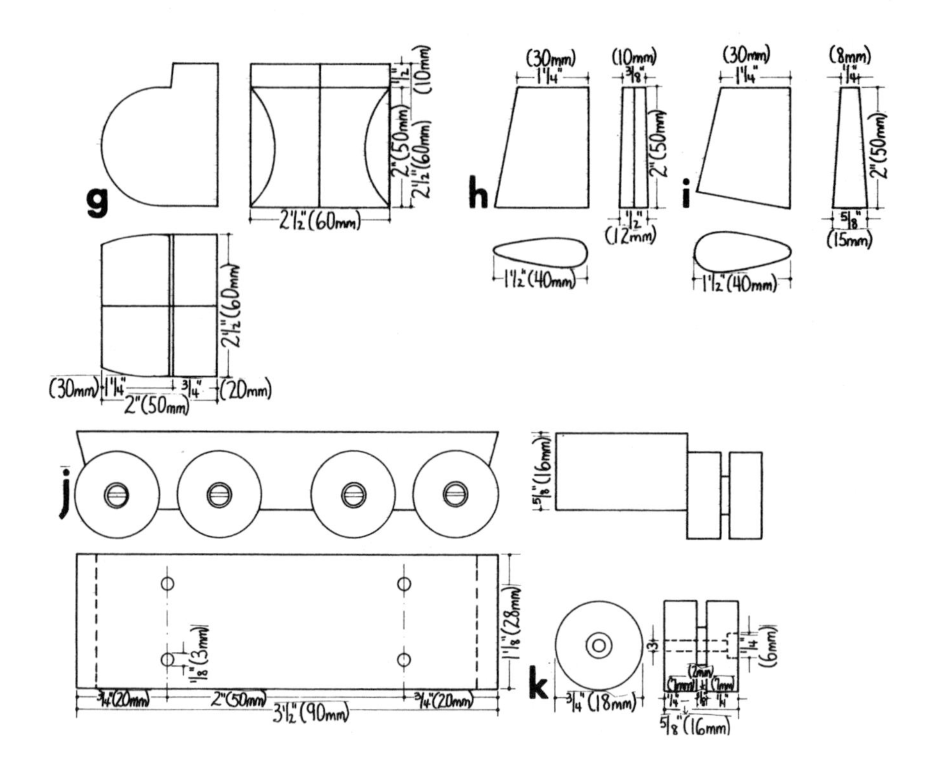

g. nose

h. elevators

i. fin

j. landing gear

k. wheel assembly

tioned in such a way that the plane neither pitches forward nor backward; therefore, a nose landing gear and a tail skid are not needed.

It is a good idea to sand the individual parts before assembly.

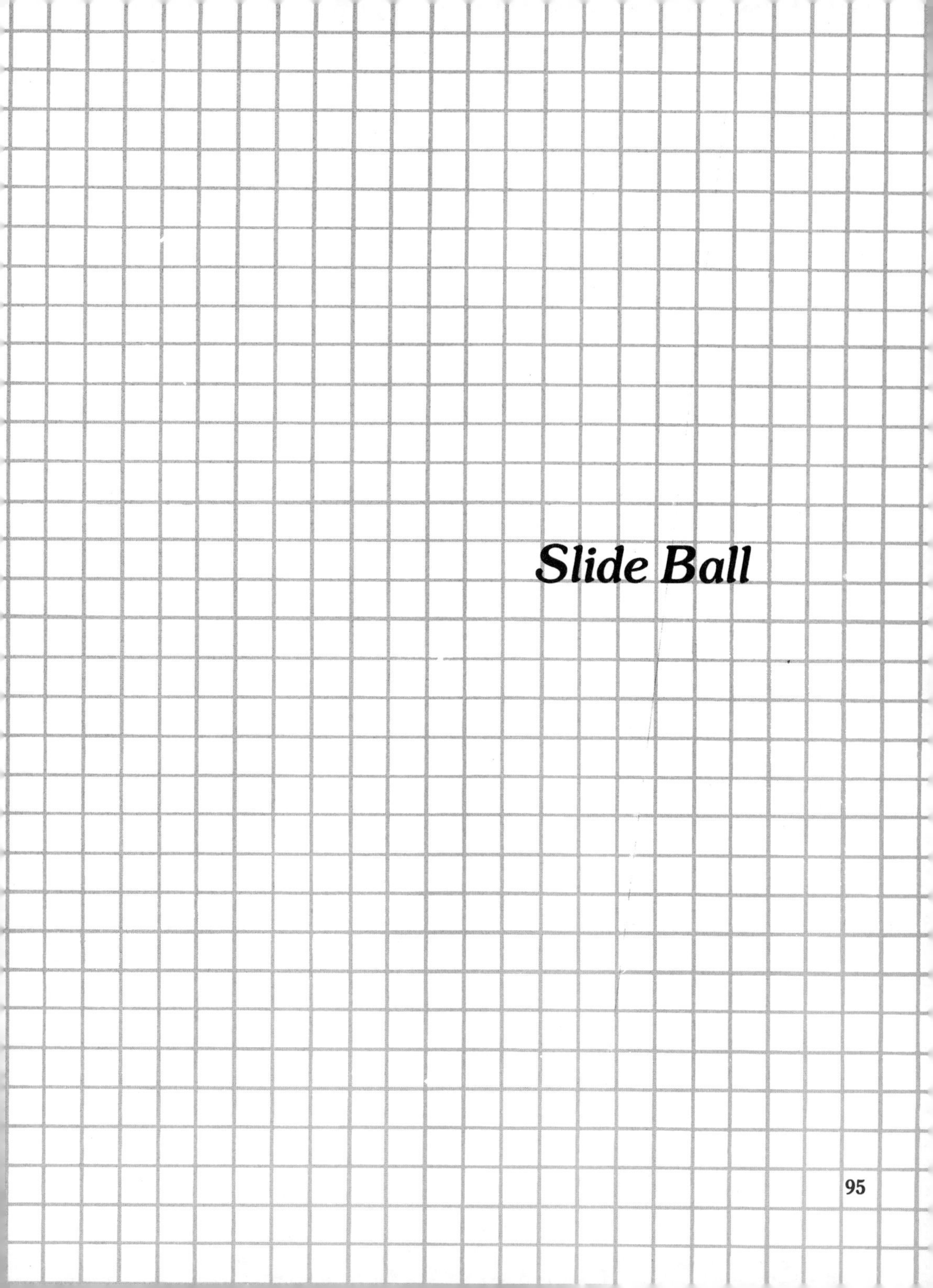

Slide Ball

Slide Ball

Young children will enjoy this simple game in which large marbles roll down sloping tracks, dropping from one to another through holes.

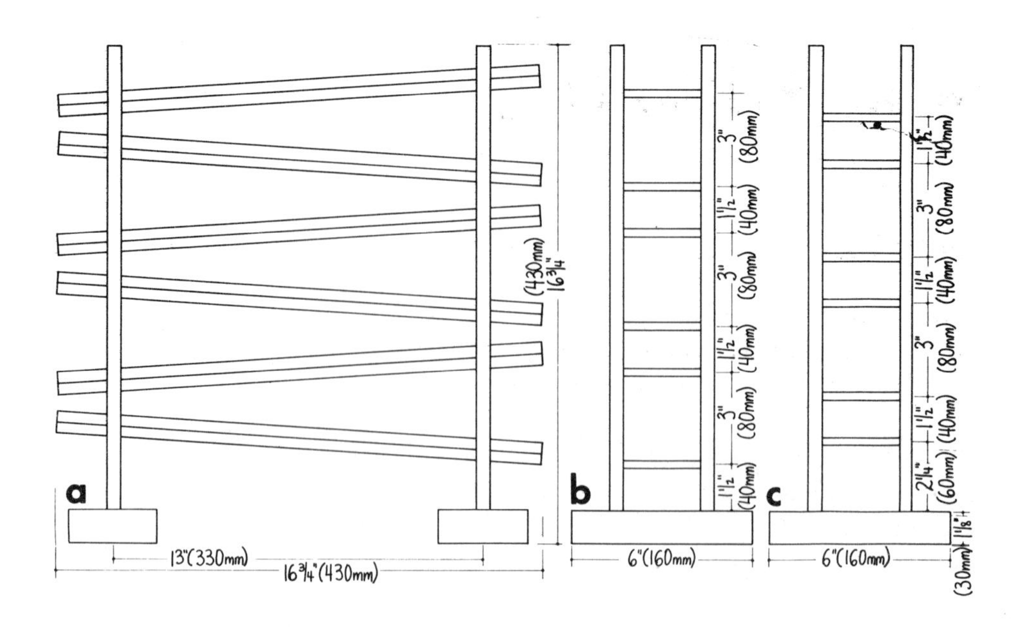

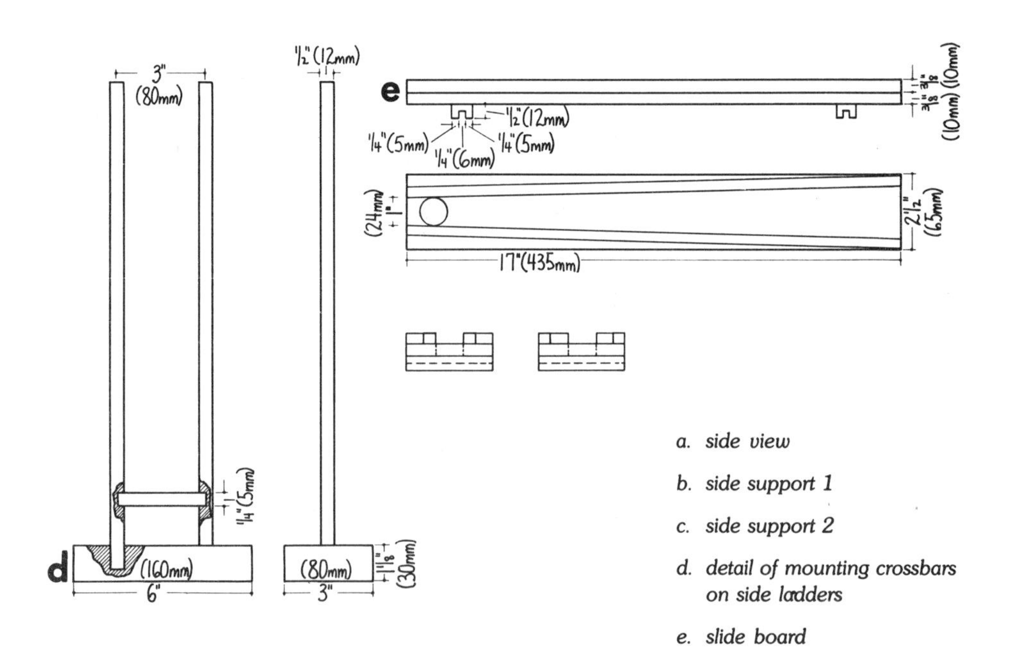

a. *side view*

b. *side support 1*

c. *side support 2*

d. *detail of mounting crossbars on side ladders*

e. *slide board*

Glue each of the side supports (**b**, **c**) into a base of solid wood $1\frac{1}{8}$″ (30 mm) thick, 3″ (80 mm) wide, and 6″ (160 mm) long.

Each side ladder has six crossbars, each 3″ (80 mm) long, made of $\frac{3}{16}$″ (5 mm) round dowels. Although the side supports are the same height, the crosspieces are mounted differently on each.

To ensure that the six holes in each of the up-

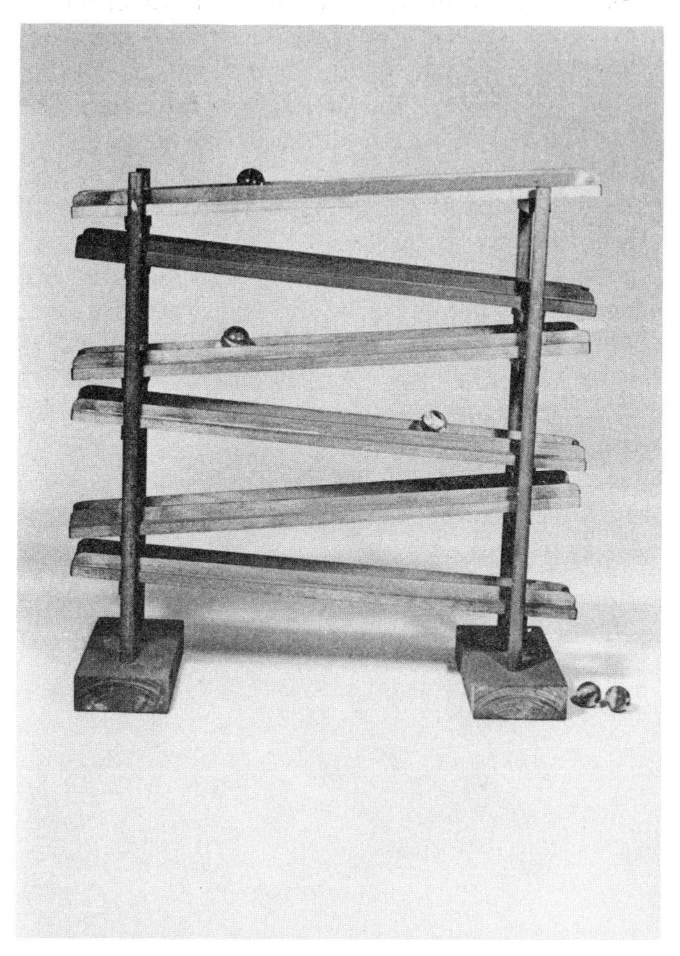

rights are aligned properly, use a drill stand and clamp the uprights so they cannot turn. Adjust the drill so that the bit goes only $\frac{1}{4}$" (6 mm) deep into the wood. Then cut $\frac{3}{16}$" (5 mm) diameter crosspieces to size and glue them into the holes. Finally, glue the finished "ladders" into the bases (**d**).

The slide boards (**e**) are made of $\frac{3}{8}$" (10 mm) thick wood. To prevent the marbles from falling off the edges, glue $\frac{3}{8}$" × $\frac{3}{8}$" (10 × 10 mm) strips on both sides of each board. At one end, attach the strips so they are at the very edge of the board. On the other end, taper the strips up to the edges of a 1" (24-mm) -diameter hole drilled in the middle of the board. This provides an alleyway that the marble slides through on the sloping board, leading directly to the hole. The marble falls through the hole and continues in the opposite direction down the next board. Place the boards so that the holes are on the lowest ends.

To hold the slide boards in place, glue small strips on the bottoms of the boards as shown in drawing **e**. The strips have $\frac{1}{4}$" (6-mm) -wide grooves in the middle that fit onto the $\frac{3}{16}$" (5-mm) -wide crossbars.

The ball slide shown in the photograph was stained *before* being glued together, since stain will penetrate only bare wood pores. Even a small amount of glue prevents staining.

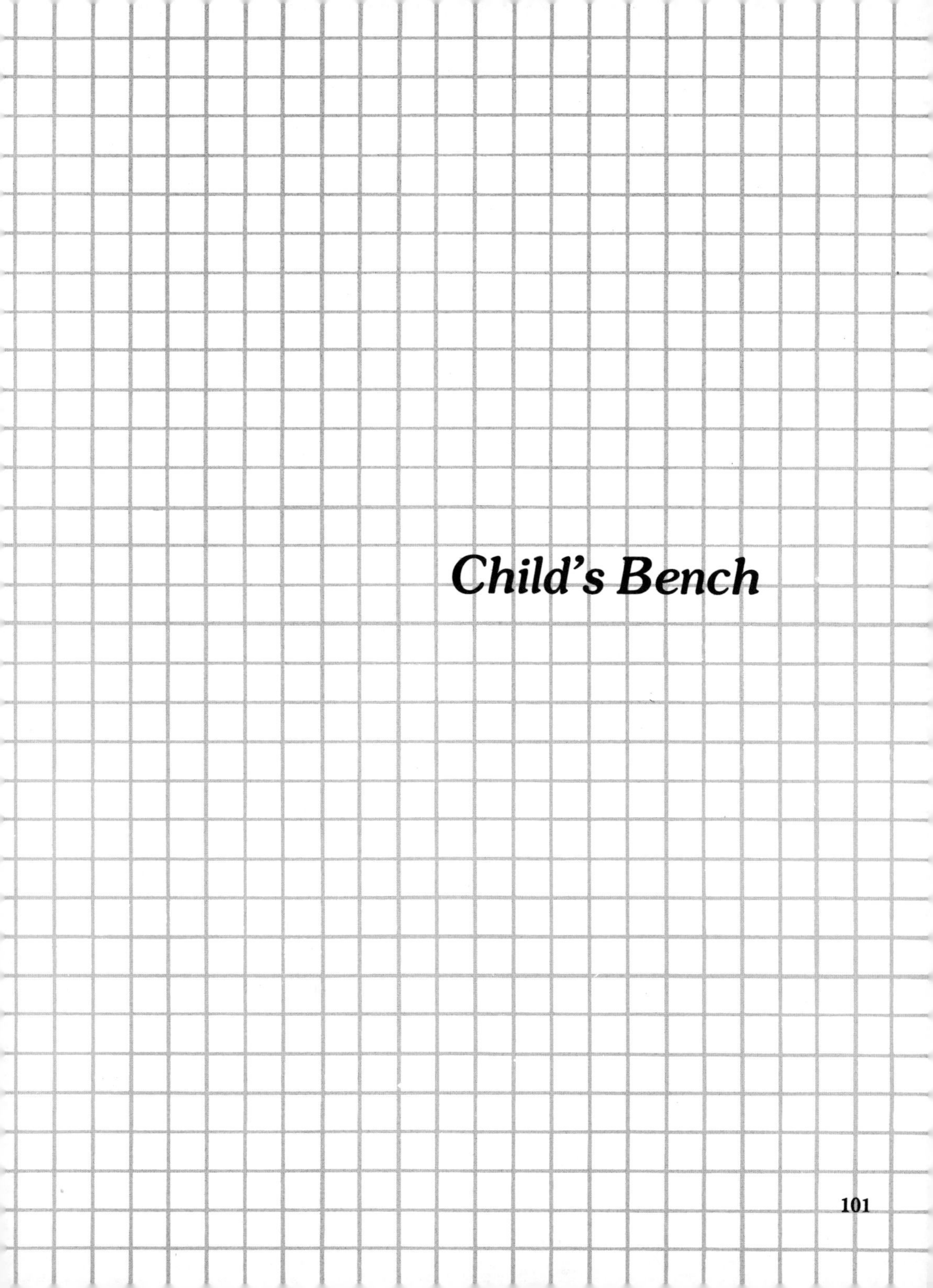

Child's Bench

Child's Bench

This bench is easy to build. The only wood needed is one board 7/8" (22 mm) thick, 8" (200 mm) wide, and 24" (600 mm) long, which you will cut into three pieces. The top part, or seat, is 12" (300 mm) long (**b**), and the supports, or legs, are 6" (150 mm) high by 8" (200 mm) wide.

Mark out the three parts on the board and make the cuts with a sharp, fine-tooth saw. Sand the cut edges so that the pieces fit together at right angles to each other.

If you butt the parts together, use dowels for reinforcement. Mark out three holes in each part for the dowels (**e**). Then, with a 7/16" (11-mm) -diameter bit, drill holes in the supports 3/4" (20 mm) deep and in the seat 5/8" (15 mm) deep. The total depth of both holes is 1 3/8" (35 mm) but it is a good idea to allow 1/8" (2 to 3 mm) for extra glue, so the dowel length should actually be about 1 1/4" (32 to 33 mm). The reason for this is that excess glue can cause a joint to burst open.

Apply glue to the dowels and in the holes in the

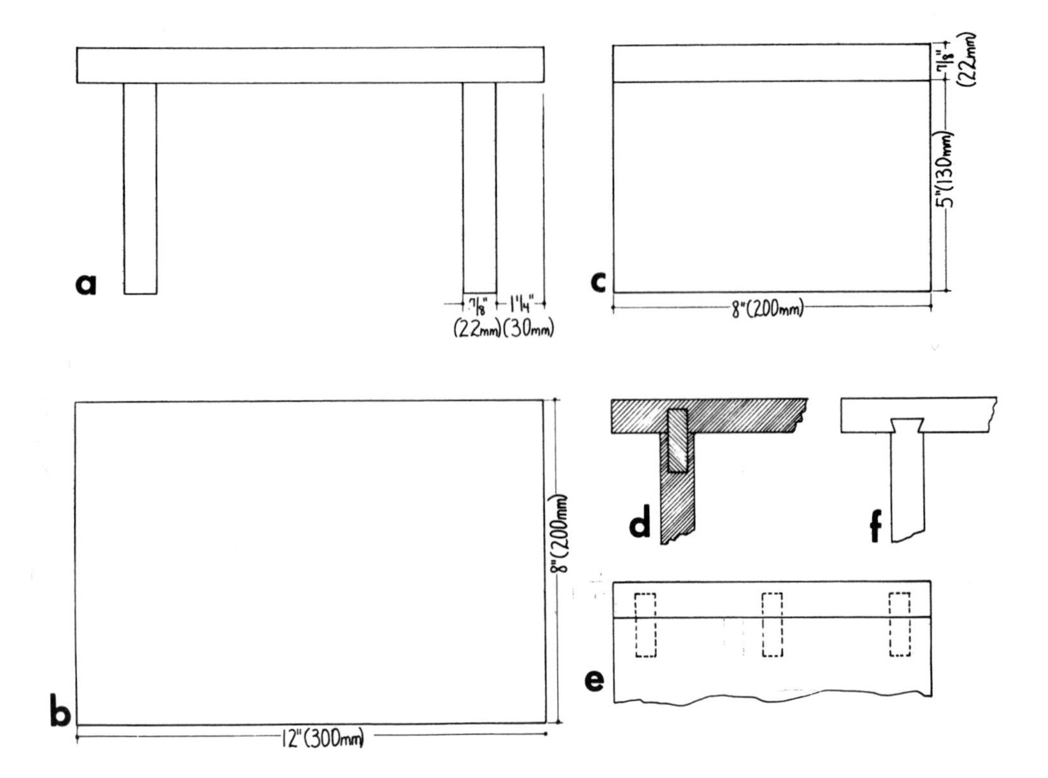

a. side view

b. top view

c. end view

d. detail of dowelled joint

e. same as "d" but front view

f. detail of dovetail joint

boards. Press the parts together with screw clamps (**d** and **e**).

If you have a router, you may want to use dovetail joints (**f**). Check the adjustment of the bit on a scrap piece of wood before working on the actual parts. The routed parts are also glued together.

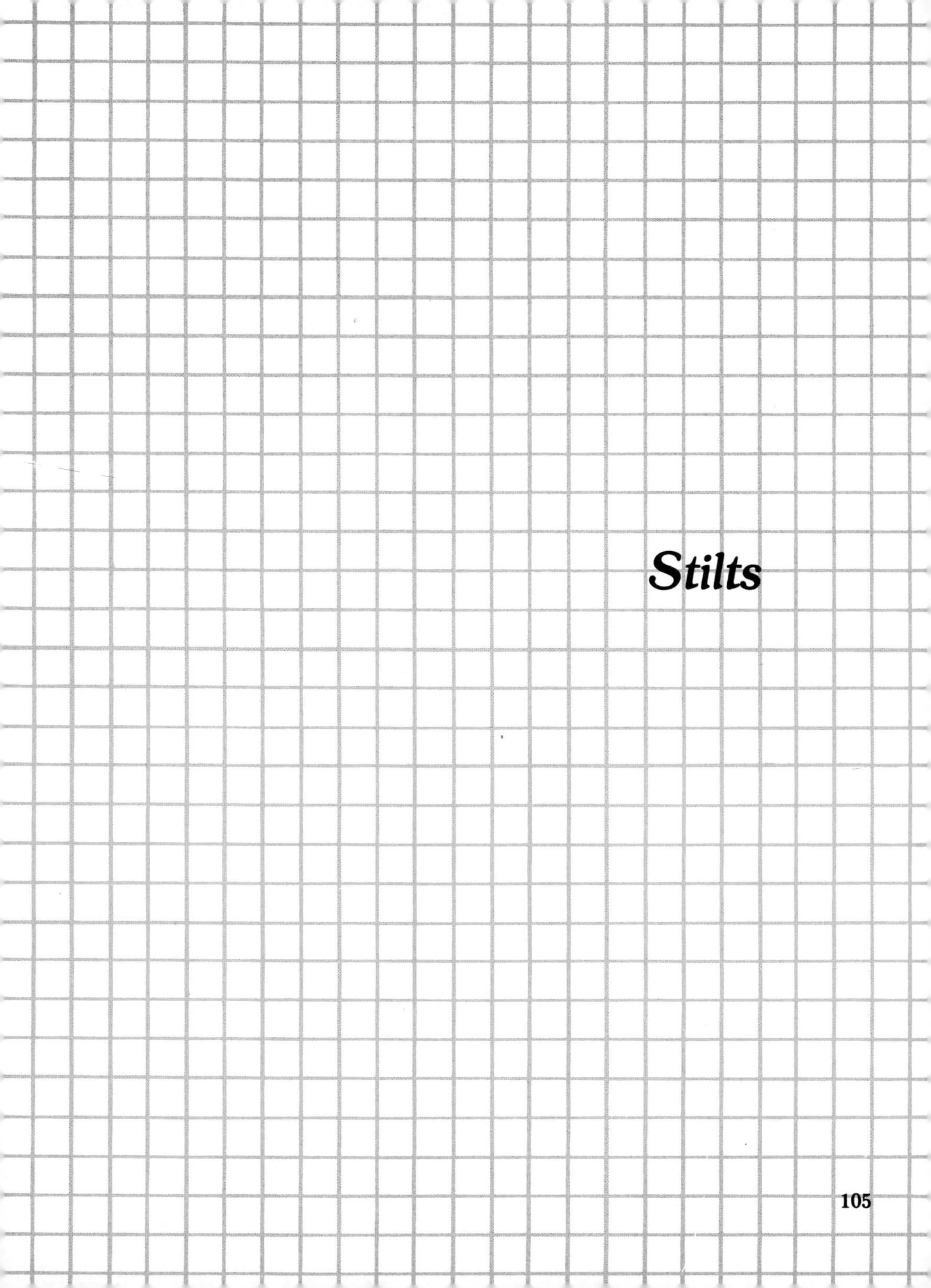

Stilts

Stilts

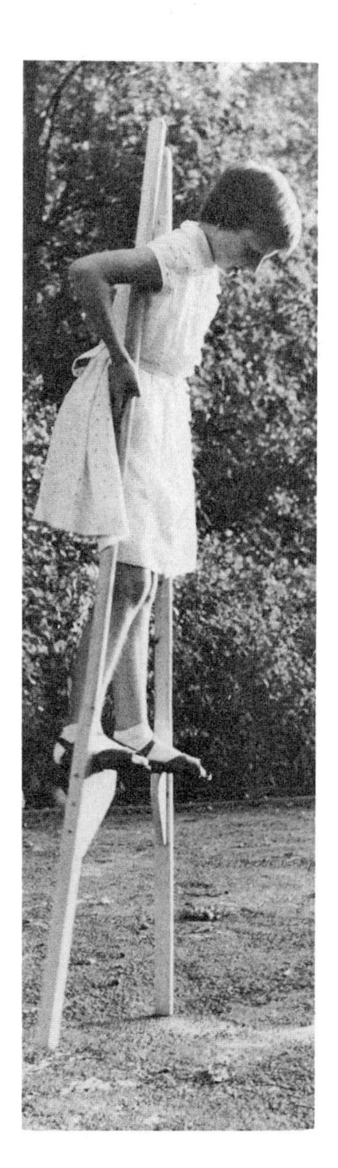

The stilts' length depends on the child they are made for. This is true for both the total length of the stilts and the height of the footrests. The dimensions shown on the drawings are right for a 5′3″ (160-cm) -tall child.

Materials needed are two 63″ (1600-mm) -long 1 ¾″ × 1 ¾″ (45 × 45 mm) pine pieces without knots. Leave the wood square-shaped up to a point 18″ (450 mm) from the top. From there taper the wood so that it comes to about 1 ½″ × 1 ½″ (40 × 40 mm) at the top. You can do this with a plane. Now round the edges with a router or a wood file.

Use a harder wood for the footrests, such as beech or ash, if you have it available. Be sure to screw, not dowel and glue, the footrests onto the stilts so that they can be reset as necessary.

If you use hardwood, the footrests may be narrower than the main piece of the stilt. In any event, after they are cut out and smoothed, mark and drill the holes first in the footrests. To begin, drill a hole with a bit as wide as the screw head, going only as deep as the depth of the screw head. Finish the hole through the wood with a bit the same diameter as the body of the screw. Place the footrest in position on the stilt and poke a nail through to mark the position on the stilt where the screw will pass through. Repeat the drilling procedure.

Start the screw from the footrest end, letting the

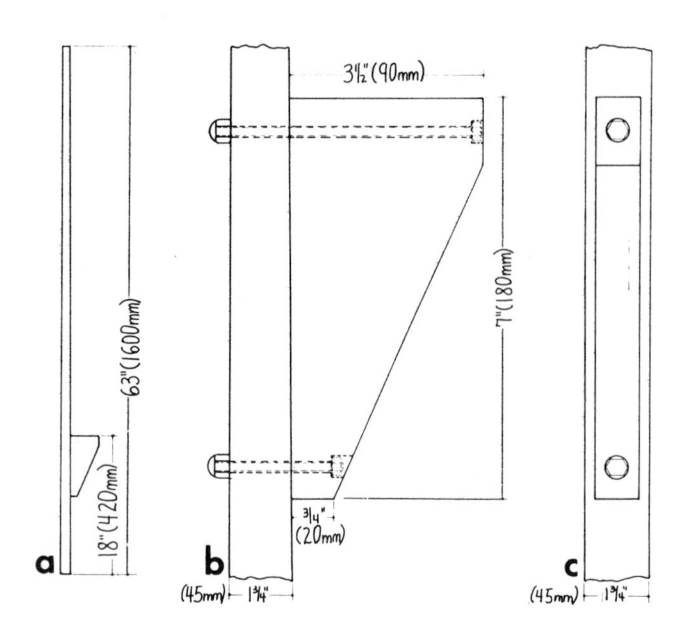

a. side view of stilt

b. detail of footrest measurements and connections

c. same as "b" but front view

nut be on the stilt end. If the screw end extends beyond the side of the stilt when you tighten it, cut off any excess with a hacksaw and file the end smooth with a metal file.

Musical Instruments

Barrel Organ

The music from this tiny barrel organ can play your favorite melody or a birthday song. The commercially available music mechanism is operated by a crank. Children love doing this.

You may have to adjust the size of the wooden case depending upon the size of the music mechanism you get.

Start by marking out the bottom piece on a $\frac{1}{4}''$ (5-mm) -thick board. This has to be large enough not only to accommodate the mechanism but also to

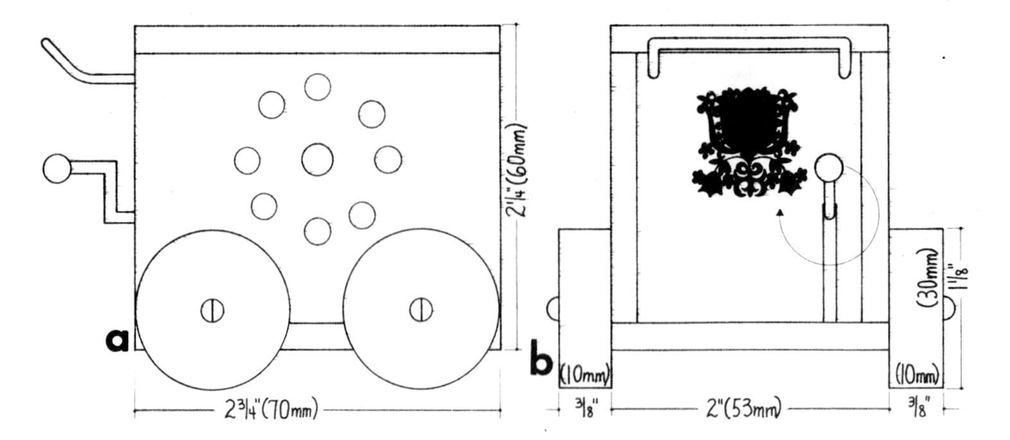

a. side view

b. rear view

allow for the width of the side panels to fit on it. Then mount the mechanism.

Next, mark out the two side and two end panels also on ¼″ (5 mm) stock. Work out on one end panel where the crank will stick out and cut a slit for it. To allow the sound to escape, drill holes through both side panels (**a**). Glue the four panels together and when dry, attach them to the base with small screws. Sand all surfaces smooth.

You can cut the wheels out of ⅜″ (10-mm) -thick wood with a coping saw. After rounding them off with a sander, drill holes through the middle of the wheels, and mount them on the case with round-head metal screws.

For the handle, bend a piece of ⅛″ (3-mm) -diameter metal rod in a vise. Glue this with epoxy resin into two holes drilled in the end panel case. For decoration, decals can be used instead of paint.

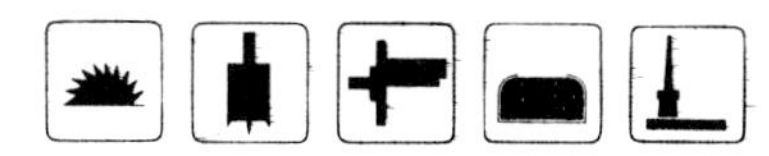

Drum and Rattle

The materials needed for these two small rhythm instruments are hardwood blocks that might be found in the scrap pile so the dimensions may need to be altered to suit what you have available. The solid block for the wood drum **a** shown is a 2″ × 5 ½″ × 1 ½″ (50 by 140 × 40 mm), finely sanded rectangle.

Now cut an opening in the block. The easiest way is to use a router to make one continuous, uniform opening, removing all of the wood to the desired depth. Alternatively use a drill with a ½″ (12-mm) -diameter wood bit to make a series of slightly overlapping holes. This has the added advantage of leaving the opening with attractive scalloped edges as shown on drawing **a**. After making the opening, slightly round the edges of the block.

The drumsticks are two ½″ (12-mm) -diameter dowels about 6″ (150 mm) long, preferably made out of the same hardwood. Smooth and finish them like the block.

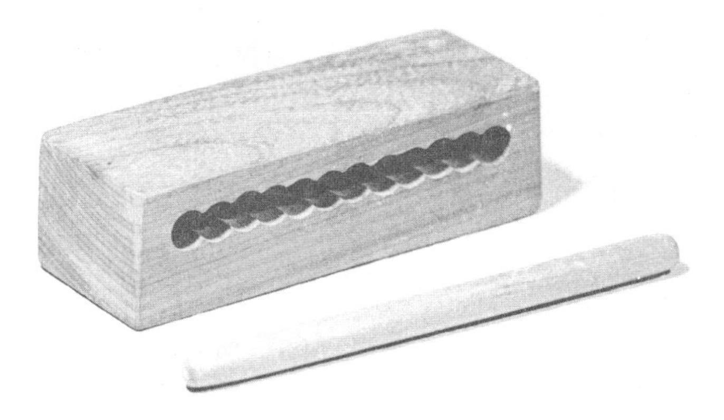

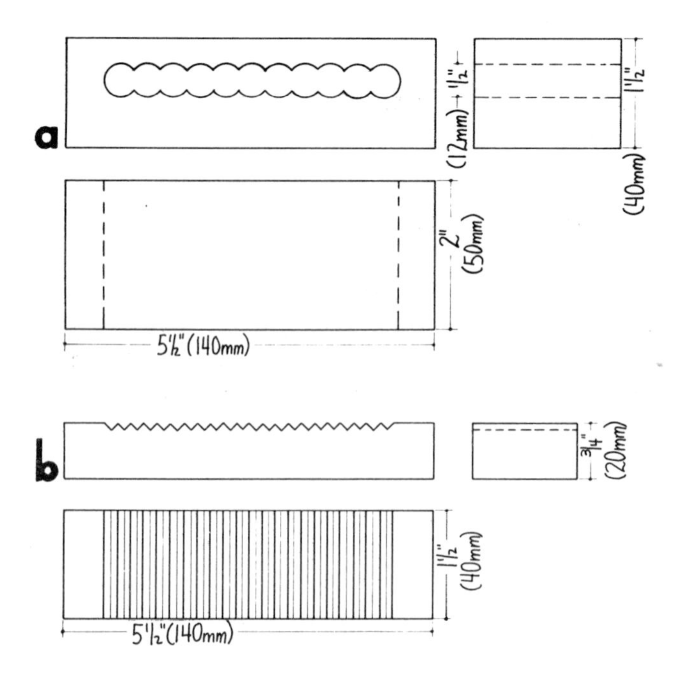

a. wood drum

b. rattle

The rattle (**b**) is also made of hardwood. The dimensions are shown on the drawing. Create the grooved surface by filing, sawing or routing.

To create sound, run a thin bar over the grooves.

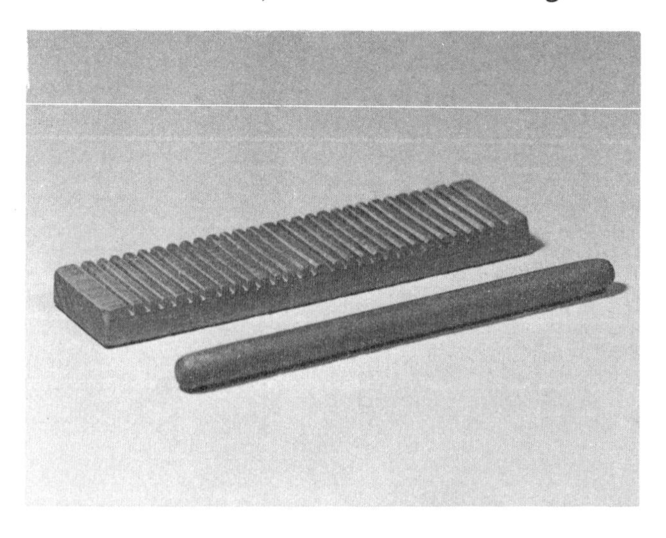

Dump Truck and Brick Cart

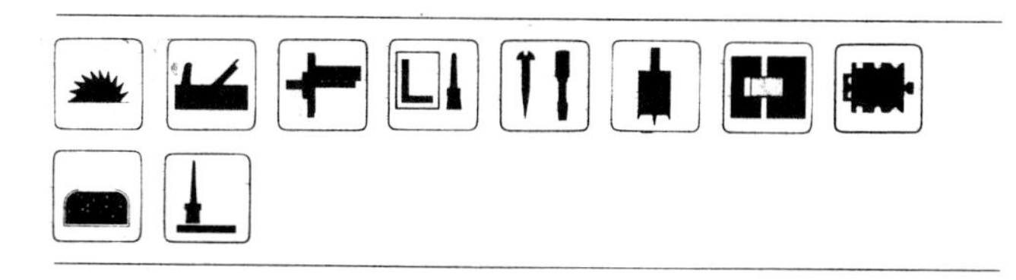

Dump Truck

The chassis is made out of two beams (**d**) and three axles (**e**), which are not only glued, but also, screwed to each other because of the weight they carry. Attach the six turned wood wheels to the axles with metal screws. Now comes the main construction. It consists of the driver's cab and the dump body.

First make the driver's cab (**g**) of one solid block of pine. If material of that thickness is not available, glue several pieces together. For extra strength, you may want to use dowels as well as glue. Shape the block as indicated and attach the finished cab to the two chassis beams with four screws.

If the driver's cab is constructed out of several layers of wood, it will look more attractive; but, a solid cab has the advantage of acting as a counterweight when the dump body is being tipped.

The dump body (**h**, **i**, **j**) is made out of $\frac{1}{4}$″ (7-mm)

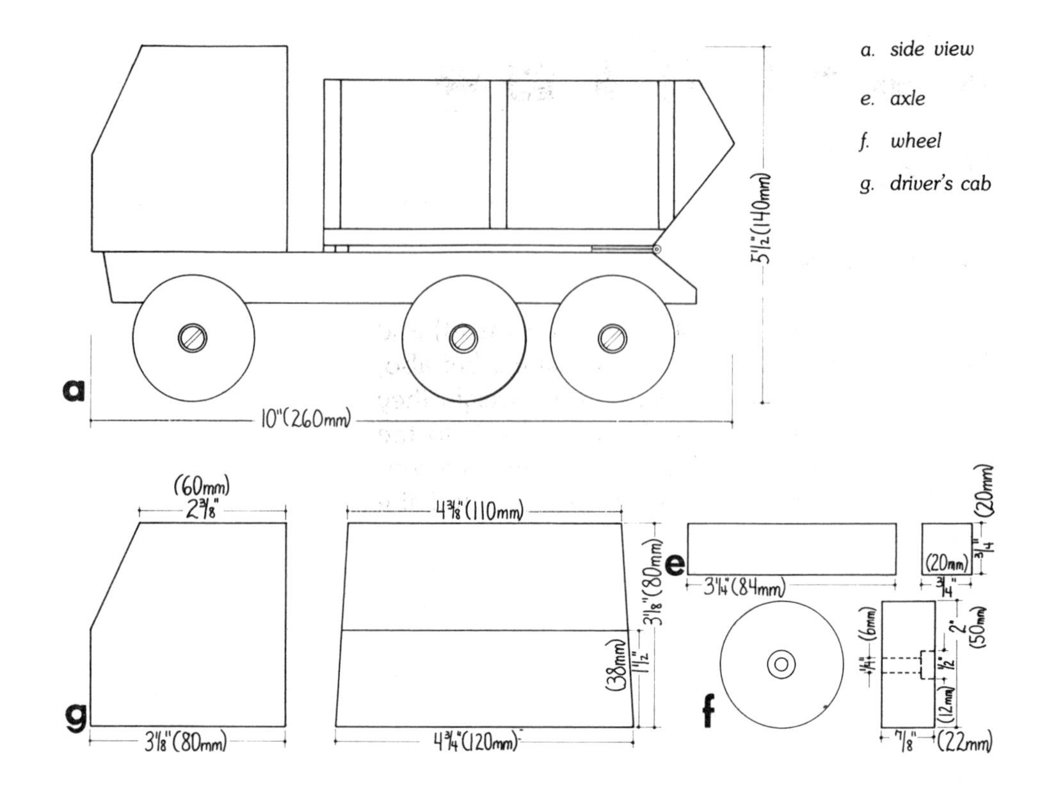

-thick sheets. Start with the bottom board and glue on the upright back panel. Then cut out six wedges, ⅝" (15 mm) wide on the bottom and 2 ½" (65 mm) high, and glue them to the bottom board as shown on drawing **i.** Against these wedges, glue the two side panels of the dump body, as shown on drawings **h**, **i**, **j** in side view and top view.

Now, only the rear panel of the dump body is left. When that is glued on and everything sanded, glue on two ½" × ¾" (12 × 20 mm) strips beneath the dump body to hold it rigid. These support strips fit exactly between the two chassis beams. Mount two hinges at the back to allow the body to tip. Now the dump truck is ready.

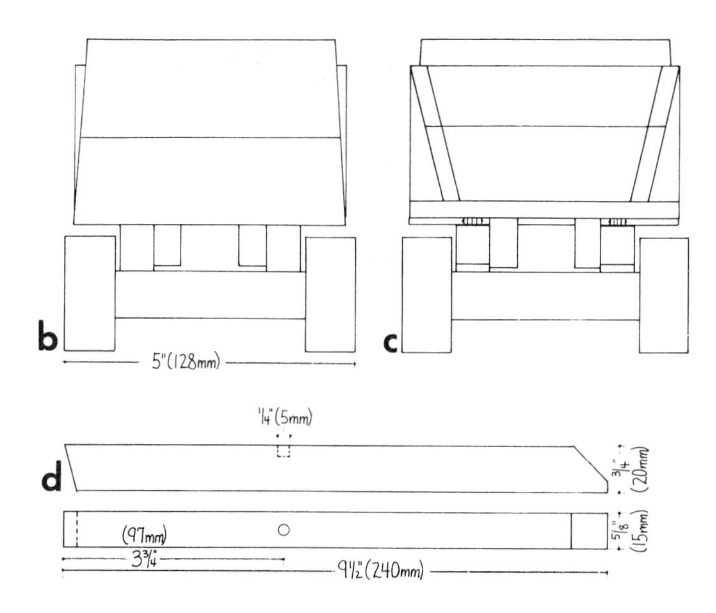

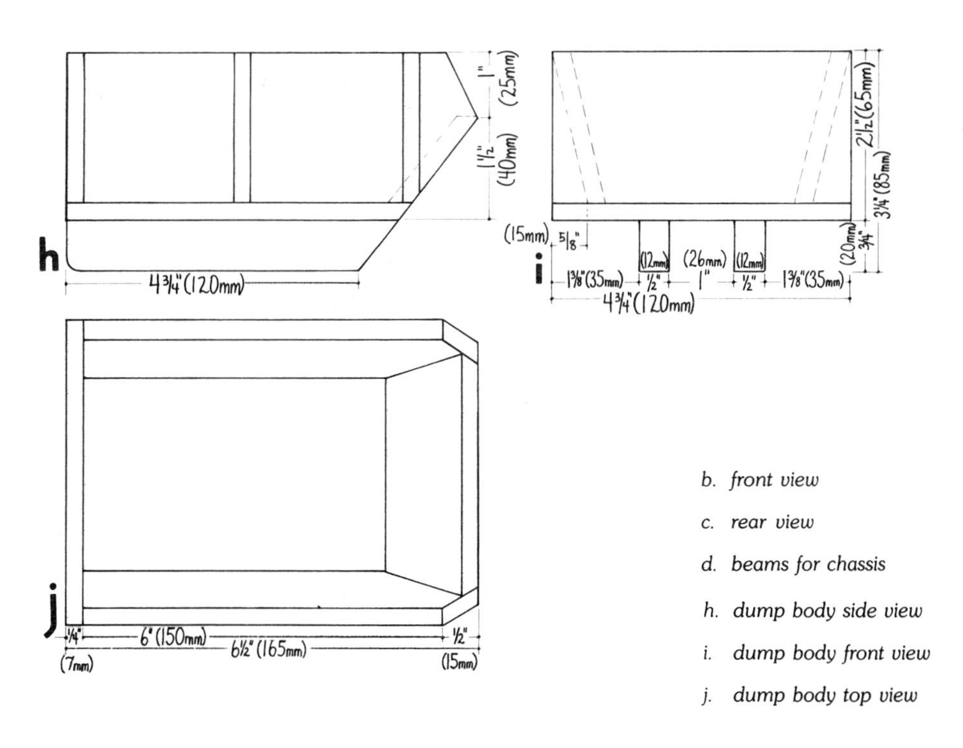

b. *front view*

c. *rear view*

d. *beams for chassis*

h. *dump body side view*

i. *dump body front view*

j. *dump body top view*

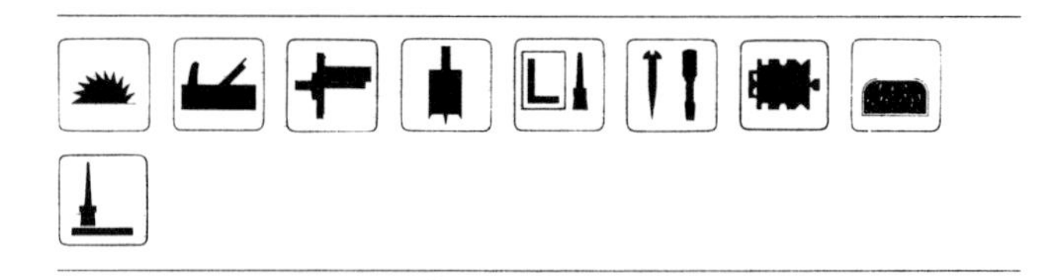

Brick Cart

This small cart is made out of $\frac{1}{2}''$ (12-mm)-thick pine and is used to haul bricks or similar loads.

Cut out five boards (**d**, **e**, **f**) with a circular saw and smooth the cut edges. Then glue the four sides (**d**, **e**) together. When dry, sand the bottom edges and glue the bottom piece (**f**) to the frame. When this is dry, sand the whole cart body thoroughly, taking care that the edges and corners remain square.

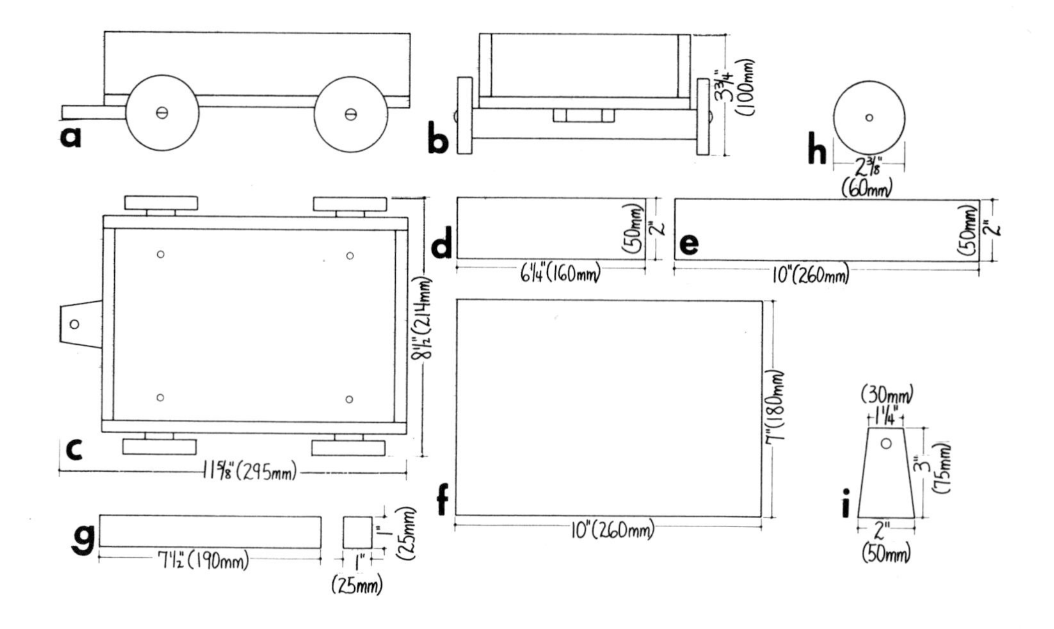

Glue the two axles (**g**) beneath the body and use two screws in each for good measure.

Now, glue and screw part **i** beneath the front of the body. Later, tie a rope through the hole for towing. The wood wheels follow. The best way to make perfectly round wheels is by turning them on the lathe. If you don't have such a machine, cut the wheels out with a coping saw. Be sure the cut-out wheels are sanded perfectly round.

There is still another way to make wheels; that is, with a hole saw. A $\frac{1}{2}$" (12-mm) -thick board is laid on a scrap piece. Fasten the hole saw into the chuck of your drill and fix the drill into a stand. Then cut the circles. The hole saw has the regular bit in the middle that serves as a guide. This will leave a hole in the middle of each wheel but this can serve to attach

a. side view

b. front view

c. top view

d. front and rear panel

e. side panel

f. bottom panel

g. axle

h. wheel

i. connection for rope

the wheel. Generally, bits are $\frac{1}{4}''$ (6 mm) diameter. Use an appropriate size screw and pre-bore a hole in the axle to prevent splitting the wood.

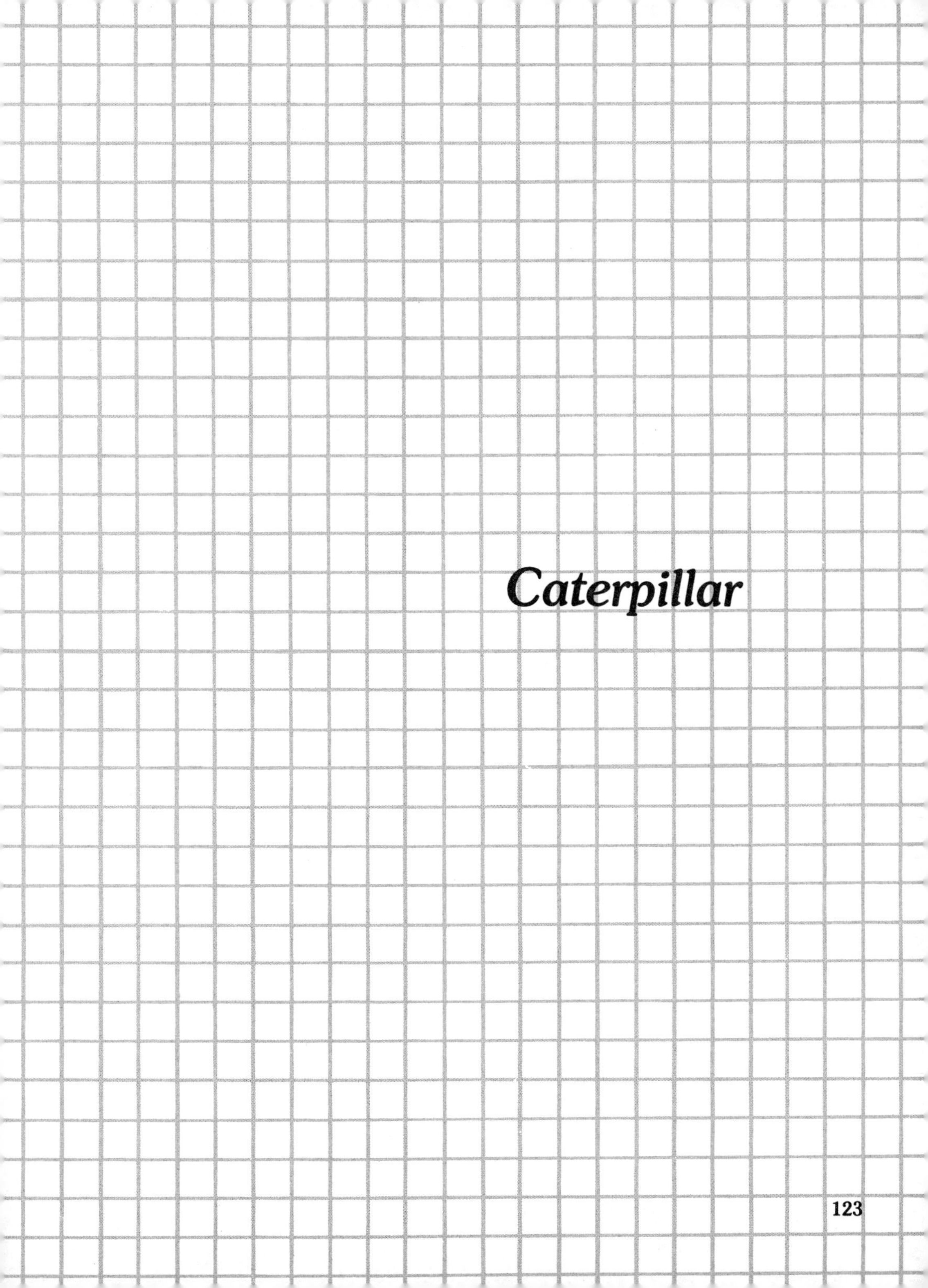

Caterpillar

Caterpillar

The caterpillar looks more complicated than it actually is. It consists of mostly identical pieces. You will need 22 wooden beads, ⅝" (15 mm) in diameter, and one larger wooden bead, 1¾" (44 mm) in diameter. The head and tail are made from the large bead. In addition, 12 wood discs, 2" (52 mm) in diameter, have to be cut from ⅝" (15-mm) -thick wood (**b**). You can cut the discs with a coping saw

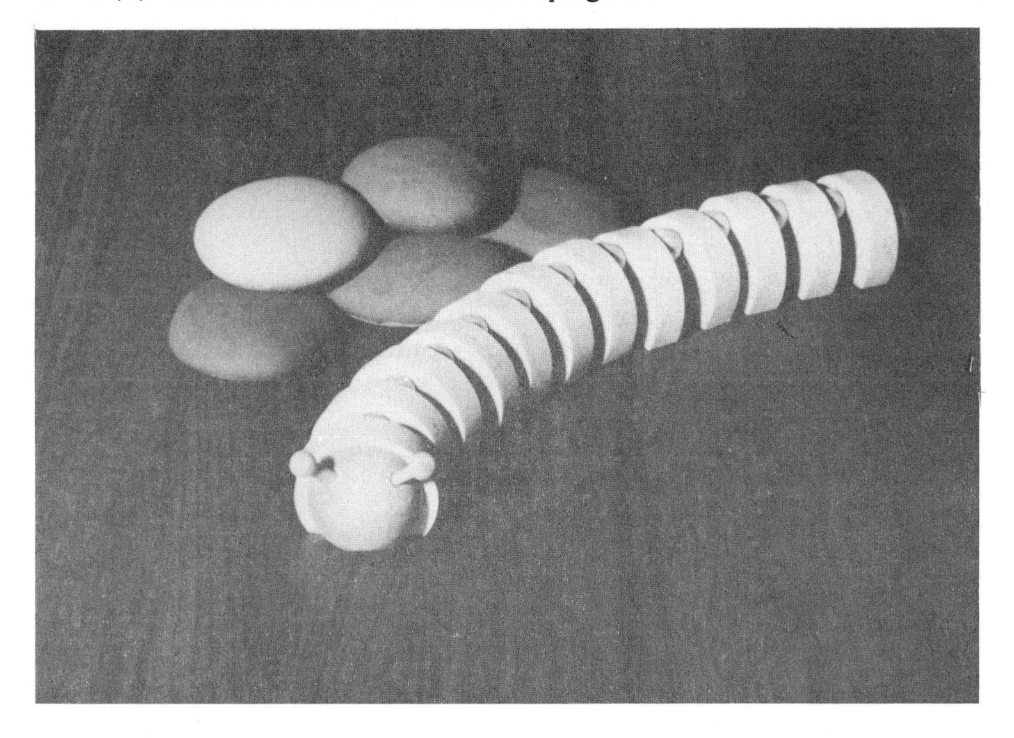

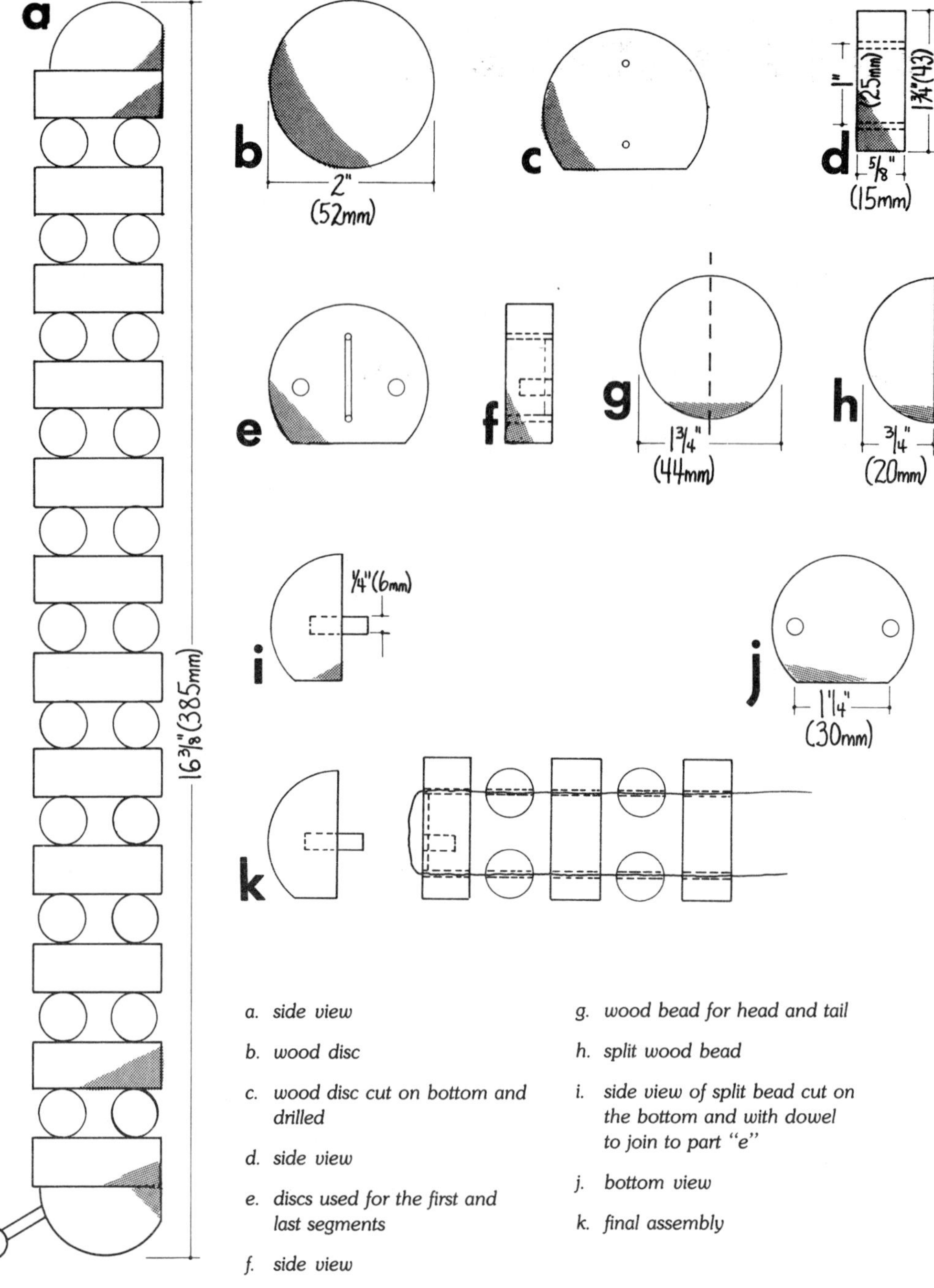

a. side view

b. wood disc

c. wood disc cut on bottom and drilled

d. side view

e. discs used for the first and last segments

f. side view

g. wood bead for head and tail

h. split wood bead

i. side view of split bead cut on the bottom and with dowel to join to part "e"

j. bottom view

k. final assembly

but it is much easier to use a hole saw fitted into an electric drill mounted on a drill press stand if you have such equipment available. You do not want a hole in the center of the wood discs so, if your hole saw is adjustable, move it down along the shaft so that there is clearance for the saw teeth to cut through the wood before the drill bit reaches it. You can also reverse the shaft, putting the threaded end into the drill chuck, using the smooth end to attach the hole saw.

When you have prepared the round discs, cut off $\frac{3}{8}''$ (9 mm) from each one (**c**). These flat edges will be the bottom of the caterpillar.

Now each disc gets two $\frac{1}{16}''$ (2-mm) -wide holes, 1″ (25 mm) apart (**c** and **d**).

The first and the last segments need some further preparation. As shown on **e** and **f**, use a chisel to remove the wood between the top and bottom holes. Keep the opening the same $\frac{1}{16}''$ (2 mm) width as the holes. When you string the segments together, pass the thread through this opening. These two segments also need two $\frac{5}{8}''$ (16 mm) diameter holes drilled $1\frac{1}{4}''$ (30 mm) apart, for the dowels you will use to connect the head and tail parts.

Cut wood bead **g** for the head and tail in half (**h**), and again cut $\frac{3}{8}''$ (9 mm) off the bottom of each. Drill two holes $1\frac{1}{4}''$ (30 mm) apart from each other (**i**, **j**) to receive the dowels attaching them to the final body segments (**e**). Make the feelers of $\frac{1}{8}''$ (4 mm) dowels with $\frac{3}{8}''$ (10 mm) wooden beads glued on the end.

Make the two feelers $\frac{3}{4}''$ (20 mm) long and glue them into $\frac{3}{16}''$ (5-mm) -deep holes at the head.

Finally, string all the parts together with sturdy cord.

Index